# Allotment Gardening

## Useful Hints and Tips for the Allotment Gardener

# Allotment Gardening

Useful Hints and Tips for
the Allotment Gardener

KEVIN FORBES

Abbeydale Press

ISBN 978-1-86147-280-9

3 5 7 9 10 8 6 4 2

Published by Abbeydale Press
an imprint of Bookmart Ltd
Registered number 2372865
Trading as Bookmart Ltd
Blaby Road, Wigston, Leicester
LE18 4SE, England

Produced by Omnipress Limited, UK
Cover design by Omnipress Limited, UK

Printed in Dubai

## THE AUTHOR

KEVIN FORBES lives in East Sussex and is an RHS
qualified gardener. He has a wide knowledge of
horticulture and likes to share this with his reader. He
says he puts his love of gardening down to his mother,
whose enthusiasm rubbed off on him. He is currently
running his own gardening and property
maintenance company.

## DISCLAIMER

These ideas are passed on in good faith but the
authors do not guarantee results, nor cannot be held
responsible for any adverse results.

# CONTENTS

# INTRODUCTION

Perhaps you live in a flat, have a small or courtyard garden, or just don't want to turn that beloved flower-bed into a vegetable patch. Whatever your reason, an allotment could be the answer to your problem.

During the 1980s and early 1990s many allotments fell into decline and owning one was associated with being old fashioned and 'not with it'! Today, however, it is a different matter. With the cost of living rising almost by the day, many people are starting to grow their own fruits, vegetables and herbs in a small attempt to become partially self-sufficient. Many young couples are now turning to allotments as it is an ideal way to eat organically without paying organic prices.

Of course obtaining an allotment can be a waiting game, especially if you live in or near a large city. In some parishes there is up to a six-year waiting list, but be patient it will be worth the wait.

Not only will your allotment garden help to keep you fit, it is also a wonderful place to meet new people. This is particularly beneficial if you live on your own and would like to meet people with similar interests. Go on and contact your local council today and get your name down on the waiting list. Winter is an especially good time to apply as most people are renewing their subscriptions at this time of year.

Here are a few small pointers to make your own plot a less daunting task:

1. Try not to be disheartened if it is totally overgrown with weeds. Think ahead and think of what you will be enjoying in the future months and years.

2. Don't expect to tackle the entire plot all in one go. Clear and dig it bit by bit and it won't seem such a mammoth project.

3. Try and get something planted as soon as possible, even it is only a single row of radishes or lettuces.

4. Start a compost heap. This will really help when it comes to treating the soil.

5. It is worth keeping an old chair at your allotment. Remember it doesn't have to be all hard work. Take time to stop for a drink and a snack, and who knows, maybe your allotment neighbours will join you.

6. Only grow the things that you will enjoy eating. There is no point in wasting your precious plot with vegetables that are not going to be eaten.

7. Finally, and probably most importantly, making your allotment growing fun. Use the time there to relax and unwind from possibly a busy day at the office or a stressful day with young children.

Once a very British hobby, allotments are now springing up in other parts of the world. People everywhere want to grow and eat really fresh food. There is nothing like eating produce that has come straight out of the ground.

# THE HISTORY OF ALLOTMENTS

It is possible to trace allotments as far back as 200 years. They started out from the Enclosure Acts of the 18th and 19th centuries. The word 'allotment' actually derives from land being allotted to an individual under an enclosures award. These enclosures were used by rich landowners in an effort to stop the peasants grazing their animals on common land. The rich benefited and food production fell into the hands of the wealthy landowners. Not only had the peasants lost their land, but they had also lost many of their common rights. By the end of the 18th century, the loss of land, combined with poor harvests, caused such poverty that there was a large section of the population that needed help.

Eventually the ruling classes came to their senses and realised that the poverty and hunger of the lower classes was starting to endanger society in general. With poverty came unrest, crime and a general breakdown in law and order. Those people who had become rich from the Enclosure Act were now being hit by a Poor Law tax, and they didn't like it.

Social reformers, such as William Cobbett, came up with the idea of giving the poor land grants. They thought that if they offered the peasants some land, it would help restore social order, reduce payments forced by the Poor Law tax, and also help alleviate the hunger by allowing them to grow their own produce.

By 1793, there was a substantial effort to provide the poor with their own plots of land. These were in the form of 'field gardens', which at the time were limited to a quarter of an acre. These field gardens were largely confined to rural areas. However, the idea was a slow starter as it coincided with improved crops and more stable food prices. Not many of the peasants accepted the offer and by 1829 there were only a total of 54 allotment sites in the record books.

## THE ALLOTMENT MOVEMENT TAKES OFF
Farm labourers hit hard times in the summer of 1830. Unemployment had reached an all time high, and many people were on the brink of starvation once again. A series of riots broke out, concentrating on the rich farmers and their brand new threshing machines. It is not surprising, therefore, that the allotment movement took off at last. Over the next 40 years, allotment sites grew to 242,542, covering almost 59,000 acres.

This success was mainly due to the LFS (Labourer's Friend Society), which was established in 1815. It promoted awareness of allotment plots and, most importantly, assisted labourers in acquiring a site. The society had their own magazine called *Labourer's Friend Magazine*, which was full of useful information on how to best employ your allotment and also made the tenancy rules clear to all.

## THE VERY FIRST ALLOTMENT
Although the subject has been a matter of much contention, it is believed the very first allotment was *c.*1795 in Long Newnton, Shipton Moyne, which is on the Gloucestershire/Wiltshire borders.

## POTATO GROUNDS
Often confused with allotments, potato grounds were in fact quite different. They were a designated area of ground purely for growing potatoes and no other

crops. Farmers gave potato grounds to their workers either for a minimal rent, or in lieu of wages. They could be either offered on a seasonal or temporary basis, and very often at times of subsistence crisis. By doing this, farmers ensured they had guaranteed tied labour at harvest times. Potato grounds became less popular as men returned from the Napoleonic Wars and, with a glut of labourers, farmers no longer needed tied workers. Eventually the potato ground became more important for the income they generated than for the labour they once provided.

## DIG FOR VICTORY

At the outbreak of World War I, allotments were needed to help grow produce for the war effort and the number of plots grew from 600,000 to 1,500,000. When the conflict was over many of the temporary allotment sites were returned to their original use.

World War II again increased the role for allotments. They were an excellent source of fresh food, especially as many of the country's farmers had gone off to fight. Allotments became a common feature in towns and cities. One of the most memorable slogans of the conflict was 'Dig for Victory', and posters started appearing everywhere. The entire British home front were encouraged to turn their back gardens into mini allotments and start growing produce. It was hoped that this would not only provide essential food for families and neighbourhoods alike, but also help the war effort at the same time.

Britain responded by turning its green and pleasant land into rows and rows of vegetables. By 1943, over a million tons of produce was being grown in gardens and allotments.

To keep the momentum going, the Ministry of Agriculture produced propagandist films to promote the importance of 'growing your own'. They made sure that literature was given to every household giving them the necessary advice, and the famous 'Dig for Victory' anthem could be heard hummed in many an allotment:

*Dig! Dig! Dig! And your muscles will grow big*
*Keep on pushing the spade*
*Don't mind the worms*
*Just ignore their squirms*
*And when your back aches laugh with glee*
*And keep on diggin'*
*Till we give our foes a Wiggin'*
*Dig! Dig! Dig! to Victory*

## A LITTLE ENCOURAGEMENT
To try and encourage children to eat more vegetables, characters were introduced such as 'Doctor Carrot' and 'Potato Pete'. These quaint characters were to try and encourage people to eat vegetables such as carrots and

potatoes in place of the more scarce commodities. The Ministry of Agriculture even suggested culinary delights such as curried carrot, carrot jam and a homemade drink called Carrolade. This was made up from the juices of carrots and swedes – yum!

Potato Pete was not to be outdone by the Dig for Victory anthem, and had his own little message:

*Those who have the will to win,*
*Cook potatoes in their skin,*
*Knowing that the sight of peelings,*
*Deeply hurts Lord Woolton's feelings.*

These comical little characters did a tremendous amount of good in getting the message across. The Dig for Victory campaign had exceeded all expectations and it was hoped that once the war was over that everyone would continue with their efforts.

Food rationing kept the demand for allotments and home grown foods going until the end of World War II, but once the conflict was over the demand dropped considerably.

### 1950 ALLOTMENT ACT
In the boom following the two world wars, more land was needed to build essential housing. This saw the re-establishment of the Allotments Advisory Body which, in 1949, recommended a scale of 4 acres to every 1,000 head of population. This decree resulted in the Allotment Act of 1950. This Act also introduced the allowance of certain types of livestock – hens, chickens and rabbits – although it has to be said many local authorities imposed restrictions of their own about what type of animals could and could not be kept on allotments.

The demand for allotments gradually declined until it reached an all-time low in the 1970s of around 500,000.

## THE GOOD LIFE

In the 1970s, there was a huge upsurge in self-sufficiency and back-to-nature lifestyle, which was epitomised by the television series 'The Good Life' which ran from 1975 to 1978. Tom and Barbara Good decide to give up the rat race and convert their garden into a mini farm. They keep pigs and chickens, and start to grow their own crops, in complete contrast to their middle-class neighbours.

However, after this major upsurge, the demand for premium building land pushed local authorities to sell allotment land for high prices to building developers.

Today, however, people are aware that something has to be done to curb ever-rising food prices and the allotment is making a comeback. There has been enormous interest from people who want to grow their own produce and more and more television programmes are being produced to encourage and advise people on how to go about it. Added to this, concerns about GM (genetically modified) foods, chemical pollution and general contamination have seen empty plots filled and waiting lists getting longer for precious allotment sites.

Hopefully this will see local authorities turning more land over to the use of allotments, so we can go back to the days of 'Dig for Victory' and stop the massive import of foreign produce. By growing your own, you are doing your part in helping to reduce global warming and reduce your own carbon footprint.

# ALLOTMENTS OVERSEAS

## GERMANY

Although allotments are considered to be a very British tradition, there is evidence of similar schemes overseas, with one prime example being Germany. This scheme is closely connected with the period of industrialisation in Europe during the 19th century. This was when many people migrated from the country to the cities in search of work and a better lifestyle. Many of these people were suffering from malnutrition and lived in inappropriate housing.

In an effort to improve their situation, local authorities and churches decided to provide open spaces for the migrants to grow their own vegetables. These were initially called the 'gardens of the poor', but were later termed as 'allotment gardens'.

This scheme reached its peak after 1864, when the 'Schreber Movement' began in the city of Leipzig. This movement was set up by a school principal Ernst Innozenz Hauschild, who established the first 'Schrebergarten' by leasing land for the physical exercise of children in a healthy environment. These areas also included gardens for the children, but it wasn't long before adults took over and started cultivating the plots.

This type of garden rapidly gained popularity not just in Germany, but in Austria, Switzerland and Sweden too.

These allotments became of prime important during the two world wars. The socio-economic situation was miserable, and nutritious food was hard to come by. It was possible to buy fresh fruits and vegetables on the black markets, but they fetched exceedingly high prices. The production of fresh produce became paramount for the survival and health of the population.

Since the hard times of the war years, the importance of allotment gardening has shifted, however. Nowadays, many of these green areas are used as recreational areas and locations for social gatherings in the middle of otherwise concrete jungles.

## SWEDEN

The first allotment garden in Sweden was established in Malmö in 1895. The inspiration behind this garden was an upper-class lady by the name of Anna Lindhagen. She had seen allotment gardens in neighbouring Copenhagen and was so impressed that she wrote a book about them. She wrote:

'For the family, the plot of land is a uniting bond, where all family members can meet in shared work and leisure.'

Anna's enthusiasm set the local authorities thinking, and they made the decision to set by certain areas for people to cultivate for their own benefit. In her efforts to advertise the importance of allotment gardening, Anna met with Lenin when he passed through Stockholm in 1917. She invited him to the allotment gardens of Barnangen to show him the full benefits, but Lenin was not impressed. He felt that workers could be better employed that 'poking around in the soil'!

The Swedish Federation of Leisure Gardening was founded in 1921. Today it represents more than 26,000 allotments and leisure gardens, which are generally leased out by the local authorities, as in Britain.

## THE PHILIPPINES

The allotment garden in the Philippines is a relatively new occupation. It first appeared in 2003, and was established in Cagayan de Oro City, Northern Mindanao, as part of a European Funded project.

With the help and encouragement of the German Embassy in Manila, this has now grown to five self-sustaining gardens. They are located in different urban areas of the city, and give access to 55 urban poor families to grow food for their own benefit.

The scheme as been so successful, they are currently setting up another four allotment gardens within the premises of public elementary schools.

The gardeners who have access to these plots grow a variety of tropical fruits, an assortment of vegetables and herbs. They are also allowed to keep small livestock and build fish ponds to give them the necessary protein sources for their dietary needs.

Each garden also has a compost heap, where biodegradable waste from the garden and neighbouring households is converted into organic fertiliser. This helps with the major problem of waste within the city.

All the gardens are also equipped with ecological sanitation toilets, similar to those used in Danish allotment gardens.

## DENMARK

When Danish architects designed housing that went upwards instead of outwards, residents found they had little or no garden. This was the background of the first allotment gardens. Many of the newer urban residents had come from the poorer rural areas and were used to cultivating their own land. They started to rent available land to grow vegetables and bit by bit managed to build small houses with any materials available.

To these people, the allotment garden became a breathing hole. Especially those that had been used to fresh air and open spaces of the country. Their spare time was at a premium, and with the garden close to their home they could make the most of the daylight hours. Sunday became 'the day' for tending to your allotment garden.

As in other European countries, the allotment became an important source of food supplies during the war. Up until World War II, allotments were fairly easy to acquire. The main criteria was that they needed to be close to home so that the tenant could walk or possibly cycle to his or her garden. When Denmark was occupied by the Germans, land for vegetable gardens was made freely available and at no cost. Many people got used to and enjoyed having the advantages of an allotment.

In 1916, the Allotment Garden Federation of Denmark was formed and gradually became an organisation with its own laws and districts. Trial plots were set aside and advisers were available to help people starting out.

When the war ended, people became more affluent and with the introduction of an annual holiday and the working day reduced to eight hours, allotments became a place for leisure, specially during the children's seven-week summer holiday from school.

The allotment garden movement peaked during World War II, with over 100,000 gardens. However, as people got richer, acquired cars and posh summer houses, the need for the allotment gardens dwindled. Motorways were extended to make space for the cars, and many allotment gardens were buried under the concrete. Those that were not destroyed were often too close to the roads and became afflicted with noise and lead pollution, making it dangerous to eat the produce grown there.

Today, however, the demand for allotments is growing all the time in Denmark, particularly in the city of Copenhagen. The solution has been for the Ministry of Agriculture to buy up any available green spaces and rent them out to the allotment garden people on a long-term basis. Organic gardening is becoming more and more popular in the allotments and many are now kept in pristine condition. Today, the Allotment Garden Federation organises around two thirds of the approximate 60,000 Danish allotments.

## CUBA

Before the revolution nearly half the agricultural land in Cuba was owned by 1 per cent of the people. After it, agriculture was nationalised and the bulk of land produced sugarcane that could be traded with the USSR for machinery, fuel, fertilizers and cheap food.

But when the USSR collapsed in 1990 — 91, Cuba's ability to feed itself collapsed with it.  People started to go hungry and radical action was needed.

The ministry of agriculture established an urban gardening culture. By 1995, Havana had 25,000 huertos — allotments, farmed by families or small groups — as well as dozens of larger-scale *organopónicos*, or market gardens. Every village in Cuba had a trained agronomist to help increase productivity and encourage children to start to grow vegetables, herbs and fruits in local school gardens. Organic growing methods were introduced and promoted and in 1996 by-laws in Havana allowed only organic methods of food production. Integrated pest management, crop rotation, composting and soil conservation were implemented. Today Cuba leads the world in many aspects of organic food production especially vermicompost (compost produced by warm farms).

# GETTING STARTED

# ACQUIRING YOUR ALLOTMENT

This is where the work begins, finding a good allotment plot! If you know the whereabouts of your nearest allotments, you should ask the plot holders how to apply for an allotment. You should find that community spirit abounds and people are only to happy to help with advice. In the absence of anyone to ask, you will probably find a notice board that may provide you with the name of the authority that provides the allotments. If you don't know where your nearest allotments are, you should contact your Parish, Town, Borough, City or District Council or enquire at your local library.

Only a decade or so ago allotments were deeply unfashionable, but now thanks to rising food prices and a better knowledge of how our food is produced many people want to grow their own produce in a way that is better for them and their environment. This was summed up nicely by the Chairman of the Local Government Association's (LGA) Environment Board:

'The last few years has seen a real upsurge in the number of people who want to get an allotment. A whole generation of twenty somethings and young families are rolling up their sleeves and picking up a trowel. Having an allotment is no longer about flat caps and thermos flasks. Nowadays allotments are the preserve of Jamie Oliver just as much as Arthur Fowler.'

At the same time as this increased demand, the LGA estimates 200,000 plots have been lost in the past three decades — an area fifteen times the size of

London's Hyde Park. This means that in many areas allotments are in short supply and there are waiting lists of up to ten years in some parts of the country. If you are put on a waiting list, confirm your interest from time to time. Allotments can be low down on the list of priorities of a parish clerk or council admin staff, so you should remind them every now and again that you haven't gone away and you still want the plot.

The 1908 Allotments Act places a statutory duty on Councils to provide a sufficient number of allotments when requested by a letter from 'six resident registered parliamentary electors or ratepayers'. So it may be worthwhile getting in touch with other people looking for a plot and see if the council meet their obligations.

There is no doubt that many allotment providers simply do not have the resources available to meet the demand for plots. This is a time for innovation and maybe you could help by suggesting areas for new plots. Is there any waste land near by? Could that a new housing estate give up a bit of land to provide a few allotments and green space? Many farms have now more or less given up on true farming and now make money from letting farm buildings for storage and light industry, surely there could be some prospects for allotments here.

The Adopt-A-Garden proposal is an inspiring scheme on the Isle of Wight. The householder who is unable to tend their garden gets it looked after for free and the gardener gets a free allotment in return. No money exchanges hands and either party can give six weeks notice at any time.

# CHOOSING A PLOT

After being on a waiting list for an allotment for eight months I was a bit surprised to be given a choice of plots. I had thought that I would be given a plot when one had became available, but in practise what often occurs is that plots are untended but not given up until the end of the subscription year, which is usually in winter. Hence the choice of plots.

If you are in the happy position of having a choice of plots there are a few points to consider:

Do you want a full-size plot or would a half plot be more suitable? Remember that the traditional 10 square rod allotment equates to 250 $m^2$ (2,690 $ft^2$) and this can be a daunting amount of work to take on for one or even two people. Most sites now provide half plots and it may be worth asking if you could share a plot.

Is the plot infested by weeds, and if so by what type and to what extent? It is highly unlikely you will acquire a weed-free plot but weeds are not always bad news. For example a few nettles or brambles and annual weeds would indicate a fertile soil but they would be relatively easy to deal with. On the other hand, perennial weeds that have rhizomes or fleshy roots such as oxalis and ground elder would be hard to eradicate, and efforts made to cultivate the soil may only worsen the problem.

What are the neighbouring plots like? If they are infested with weeds, there may not be anything you can do about it and your newly cultivated plot would be plaqued by the seeds from these plots.

How easily is the plot accessed? You may wish to transport a significant amount of manure, a shed and/or a rotovator to your plot — if so ask yourself — how would you get it to your plot?

How near is the water supply? You will spend a lot of time watering your vegetables, and water butts would be a good idea, however you may have to rely on the sites' water supply a lot of the time.

Keep security in mind when choosing your plot. Sadly vandals and thieves do strike allotments from time to time so bear in mind that a plot that is overlooked by passing traffic or by neighbours may be less prone to attack than one hidden away out of sight.

Most crops require a good supply of sunlight so avoid sites shaded by large trees. Bear this in mind if you are viewing your plot in winter and envisage the trees nearby in full leaf. Small trees and hedges are good as they would provide some protection from strong winds. If any of your crops do require to be grown in part shade, this can be provided by netting or growing plants such as runner beans and Jerusalem artichokes.

If you are in the happy position of not only being able to choose between plots but also between sites, here are a few more points to consider:

Is the site a statutory site? A statutory site has been acquired specifically for use as allotments and cannot be sold or used for other purposes without the consent of the Secretary of State. Temporary and privately owned are not protected from disposal in the same way as statutory sites.

Does the site have an allotment society? Not all sites have societies and the purpose and responsibilities of these societies can vary widely. Some sites are managed by the allotment society and every plot holder can have a say in the running of the site. You will probably find that these "self-managed" sites are more likely to have better facilities and possibly the plots will be tidier as they may be required to be kept to a certain standard by the commitee.

Other societies do not manage the site but exist more to provide mutual help among plot holders, through seed exchange and bulk purchase of items such as fertilisers.

Many sites have toilet facilities, clubhouses, site huts and/or sheds provided. Obviously all these facilities are advantageous.

Security measures will vary from site to site, some being well fenced and under lock and key, others being open to all and sundry. Generally speaking these measures are more in need in urban rather than rural areas.

# IMPROVING THE SOIL

Once you have managed to acquire an allotment, you will probably have itchy feet to get started. Your plot may not have been attended to for many months and there is a real chance that it will be totally overgrown. So where do you start?

The very first thing to do is to check what type of weeds are growing on the plot. If there are a lot of nettles, docks, buttercups and daisies, the probability is that your soil is acidic. If the weeds are lush, this is in fact a good sign and means that your soil is fertile. If they are sparse and frail looking, then it generally indicates the soil will need quite a lot of work.

## USING A ROTOVATOR

In their enthusiasm to get the plot ready for growing produce, many newcomers to gardening will resort to hiring or borrowing a rotovator and turn over the entire plot straight away. Not a good idea! Many weeds are able to grow from a tiny fragment of their roots, so chopping them up and tilling the soil is an ideal way to ensure that your new plot will be absolutely covered in lush weeds in just a few weeks time.

A rotovator is a good tool for breaking up heavy compacted soil and creating the fine tilth required for sowing seeds but the weeds have to be dealt with first.

For those of you who do not choose the organic route, the best way to attack the weeds is to spray the area with a reliable systemic weedkiller such as Roundup. When the tops have all withered, then is the time to rotovate the soil. This sounds very simple, but you do have to bear in mind that you will be growing your vegetables in ground that has been treated with a chemical. Also to be effective, the weedkiller has to be applied when the weeds are actively growing, so not in late autumn and winter.

You can avoid the use of weedkillers and be sure that your produce is untainted by chemicals. It takes time and a bit of hard work but will be worth it. Tackle as large a part of the plot as you can manage by digging out perennial weeds, making sure you take out all of the roots. To keep the rest of the plot under control until you are ready to cultivate it, make use of sheet mulches of layers of newspaper, cardboard or black plastic sheeting. After you have cleared each section of perenial weeds, you can then turn them over with a rotovator, incorporating rotted manure or compost at the same time.

## MANUAL DIGGING

Digging by spade, fork or digging hoe helps to provide good conditions for plant growth by aerating the soil. On heavy soil digging helps improve drainage and the soil structure. At the same time weeds can be taken out and organic matter and/or fertiliser added.

The best time to dig over the plot is autumn because the following winter frosts will help to further break down any remaining clods. Do not dig heavy soil when it is wet because this may only damage the soils' structure.

There are a number of different methods to digging:

### Simple digging
This is as it implies, lifting a spadeful of soil, turning and dropping it in the same spot it came from. Weeds can be taken out and organic matter added as required.

### Single digging

This is a more methodical approach where a plot is dug over to spades depth (a "spit") one trench after the other. Start at one end and dig out the first trench, leaving the soil on the ground, the opposite side of the next trench to be dug. Take out weeds as you go. If neccesary incorporate organic matter, lime and/or fertiliser to the bottom of the trench and when digging the second trench turn the resulting soil and drop it into the first trench. Proceed with the following trenches in the same manner, and fill the last trench with the soil from the initial trench.

### Double digging

Double digging is suitable for improving plots with poor drainage. The soil is worked to two spits deep. It is important that while double digging that subsoil is not brought to the surface or mixed with the top soil. As with single digging, double digging is done in trenches. When the first trench is dug, turn over the soil in the bottom of the trench and then shift the soil from the second trench into the first, adding any soil improvers as required. If you have a good supply of organic matter, digging this into the bottom spit will help improve drainage.

### SOIL ADDITIVES

For plants to flourish, they need a soil with good structure in which required nutrients are not only present but also available to the plants' roots. A well structured soil is not compacted, and water, air and nutrients circulate through it. To improve a poor soil, incorporate matter that opens the structure and help form crumbs of soil.

Organic matter including well rotted manure and garden compost improves any type of soil structure and also provides nutrients. Other types of additive are suitable only for specific types of soil: poor drainage in a heavy clay soil can be helped with gravel, grit or sharp sand but it would require a large quantity.

## Manure

Manure contains few nutrients if it is compared directly to inorganic fertiliser weight for weight but this would be a simplistic comparison. Manure not only adds nutrients but its bulky nature improves the structure of the soil and this makes these nutrients more readily available to the plants roots. Additionally manures usually come with the added benefit of micronutrients that might not be present in inorganic fertiliser. When you start cultivating your plot, manure might well be the most suitable additive to help improve your soil because it will take a few months for your compost heap to start producing. Make sure it is well rotted before adding to the soil, as fresh manure burns plants and actually creates a nitrogen deficiency in the soil while it rots down. This is especially true of horse manure, which often contains bedding materials such as straw or sawdust. Store fresh horse manure at least six months before adding it to soil. Try to make sure that the manure is from a trusted, preferably organic source because there have been instances of manure being contaminated with weedkiller.

## Garden compost

One of the first things you need to position on you plot is your compost bin or heap. It takes a while for your heap to start producing but it may be possible to start adding garden compost as soon as you start cultivating your plot. All councils are now obliged to recycle as much waste as is possible and this includes garden and other organic waste. Much of this organic waste is turned into and in some areas is available in bulk quantities to the general public. Contact the environment department of your council to get more information.

Position your compost bin in a sunny, sheltered position as warmth speeds up the process. Compost bins are available from DIY stores, garden centres and sometimes may be supplied by local authorities at discounted rates. You can also make you own, and for a very simple and quick bin, hammer 4 wooden stakes in the ground a metre (3 ft) apart, to form a square, fix wire or plastic netting around the stakes, and line with cardboard.

The key to making a good compost bin or heap is to create good air circulation by using a mixture of finer materials (grass clippings, leaves etc) and coarser materials (shrub clippings, straw etc). This mixture prevents the heap from compacting. Regular turning of the compost bin with a garden fork (once or twice a month) speeds up the composting process. Most of the vegetable waste may be composted but not pernicious, perennial weeds or weeds in seed.
The compost will take about three months to be ready to use. Good, ready-to-use compost material will be crumbly and brown, damp but not wet and not smell unpleasant. Sieve through the compost with a garden fork and take out any uncomposted material. This can be put to one side chopped up with a spade and added to the next batch.

Digging the compost into plant/vegetable beds is the best use of compost, because this will improve the soil texture and provide a long-lasting supply of slow release nutrients. An alternative is to use the compost as a mulch.

## Mushroom compost

Spent mushroom compost is low in nutrients but still good for lightening heavy soil, and the lime it contains will reduce the acidity of soil. You can sometimes find it in garden centres, but it will be cheaper if you can buy it directly from a local mushroom farm.

## Green manures

These are fast-growing plants grown specifically to be dug back into the soil to provide nutrients. Also while they are growing, they suppress weeds and are ideal for vacant areas that are in between crops. There are green manures that are suitable for summer or winter. All green manures should be dug in before flowers form and while the stems are still soft so that the plant can break down easily without taking nitrogen from the soil. If used in a rotation system, check the family of plants being used. Red Clover, for example, being a legume, would fit into a rotation in place of beans, and would be followed by a leafy vegetable such as spinach or lettuce.

Summer green manures to try include mustard and rape, which will be ready to dig in four to six weeks after sowing, however mustard has the disadvantage that it is liable to get club root, and so keep the disease going in the ground.

Essex red clover can be sown from spring through to autumn. Because it is a member of the pea family, it takes nitrogen from the air and releases it through its roots into the soil. Leave a few plants to flower as they attract bees.

For winter specific manures, include grazing rye, which releases compounds that inhibit germination of seeds and winter field beans which are another nitrogen fixer, best on heavy soil.

## Concentrated organic fertilisers

Bone meal, seaweed meal and blood, fish and bone are concentrated organic fertilisers; they are easy to use and store and are consistent in proportions of nutrients. They provide a slow release of nutrients but are relatively expensive.

## Inorganic fertiliser

Containing high percentages of a given nutrient, these feeds can provide a quick boost to deficient plants. Because they are so concentrated, overuse may harm soil organisms. If you use them, apply sparingly but frequently, not in one large dose.

## Lime

Liming is required to grow certain vegetables (such as cabbages) on acidic soil. Lime may be spread on the soil at any time of year but needs to be done so as far in advance of planting as is possible. Do not add lime at the same time as manure because the two react against each other. It is best to apply lime and manure in different years appropriate to your crop rotation plan. If you soil is not to acidic, using mushroom compost may be a more gentle way of raising the soils pH.

# THE PRINCIPLES OF CROP ROTATION

The principle of crop rotation is to grow specific groups of vegetables on a different piece of land every year. These groups are moved around so that they don't grow in the same spot for at least three years.

Because pests and diseases tend to attack specific plant families, by rotating crops you can help to break the life cycle and alleviate a build-up of the problem.

Crops such as potatoes and squashes are good ground coverers and help to suppress weeds, which will minimise the problem for the following crops.

Because different crops require different soil conditions, by changing the crops every year, you will minimise overuse of the soil and allow it to replenish itself. Also soil structure can be improved by alternating deep-rooted and fibrous-rooted crops.

## HOW TO WORK YOUR ROTATION

Divide your vegetable plot into four or five equal sections, for this example I am using four. Decide which crops you want to grow and then group them depending on their soil requirements (see opposite). Decide which crops you would like to grow from each group and then work as follows:

| | | | |
|---|---|---|---|
| Year one: | GROUP A | GROUP B | GROUP C |
| Year two: | GROUP B | GROUP C | GROUP A |
| Year three: | GROUP C | GROUP A | GROUP B |

**GROUP A**
aubergines
beetroot
carrots
celeriac
celery
courgettes
cucumbers
garlic
leeks
marrows
onions
parsnips
peppers
potatoes
pumpkins
salsify
scorzonera
shallots
tomatoes

**GROUP B**
broad beans
chicory
endive
French beans
lettuce
peas
runner beans
spinach
Swiss chard
sweetcorn

**GROUP C**
broccoli
Brussels sprouts
cabbages
cauliflowers
kale
kohlrabi
turnips
radishes
swedes

**GROUP D**
any crops that need to
stay in the same piece
of ground undisturbed,
such as:

asparagus
currants
globe artichokes
gooseberries
rhubarb

# SHEDS AND TOOLS

# THE SHED

An allotment plot without a shed just does not seem quite right. Although usually very practical, they can on occasion be just a little eccentric and fun and are often artistically made from recycled materials with great ingenuity and imagination.

You may be lucky enough to have a shed already in position for your use on the plot. If not, you will need to consider early on in the planning of your plot as to whether you want a shed and where you will site it. However before deciding to buy or build a shed, you will need to consult the allotment sites regulations as there is most likely to be some rules regarding buildings on you plot. The size, materials used, position, how many sheds or other structures you may have, if at all, may all be mentioned in the rules.

The shed could be used for storing tools and other sundry items such as seed trays and pots, cloches and fleece, twine and labels. There are many items that are useful to have at hand when you need them, not back at home. The shed can also can provide shelter from bad weather or a place for a ten-minute break from your toils.

Wait for the sales and you can buy a £100 shed from your local DIY store, but if you have the spare time available you could build a far stronger shed from recycled materials, saving money and of course saving the planet at the same time. I have seen sheds made from upturned boats, redundant horse trailers and many made from the corregated metal sheeting that was once used for air raid shelters.

If you like the idea of building from recycled materials, an ideal source of free strong timber is the humble pallet. There are many of these pallets lying around outside factories and warehouses, some being stored for future use, but in many cases there will be some that are surplus to requirements, just ask first before taking. You can use this pallet-wood to strengthen an existing shed, as part of a new build shed or for the entire shed.

Security is an issue you need to consider. If theft and vandalism is common at your site, it may be best to have a metal shed. Spend the bare minimum on your shed but have a decent closed shackle padlock on a hasp attached to a secure mounting point. The hasp itself should also have concealed fixings or recessed bolts. An alternative is a mortice-style lock specifically for sheds. DIY store sheds are usually made from the flimsiest of materials, so consider strengthening these sheds with recycled timber. The window is usually a weak point on a shed, and a removable shutter on the inside would provide more security and prevent thieves from seeing what is stored inside. When choosing a site for your shed, choose a spot that is not hidden from view.

The other aspect of security of allotment sheds is not to store anything here you cannot afford to lose. Do not keep your best, most treasured or expensive tools here — store them at home. Keep an allotment set of tools at your plot. These adequate but cheap tools can be second-hand, ones you can find these at boot fairs and charity shops or new from a DIY stores' own brand.

# GREENHOUSES AND FRAMES

Before acquiring a greenhouse, consult the regulations as to whether you are allowed to site one on your plot. You may find you are allowed either a shed or a greenhouse but not both. There may also be rules about the size and what materials it is constructed from.

### Greenhouses

A greenhouse on your plot will extend your growing season, providing a place to bring on young plants and to grow tomatoes, peppers, cucumbers and grapes. In winter there are plenty of salad crops to grow, including winter lettuce, rocket, parsley and radish. The downside of a greenhouse is that it will involve more tasks, and you may need to visit your plot more often. Obviously it will require regular watering and some plants will prefer a humid environment. Shading and ventilation will be required in hot conditions. To keep pests and diseases to a minimum, the greenhouse must be kept clean and free from dead leaves. At least once a year, preferably on a mild day in early winter, clean and disinfect the entire greenhouse. Use a proprietary window cleaner on dirty glass, a plastic plant label is good for cleaning between panes. Staging and other surfaces should be sterilized with garden disinfectant.

Site the greenhouse in a light position but also one that is sheltered from wind. If the greenhouse is mainly to be used for summer crops, align it with the longer axis running north to south. If it is to be used mainly for bringing on young plants in spring, align it east to west as this would make the best use of available light.

Very often second-hand greenhouse can be found for very little money or even given away. Check your local advertising paper or the recycling web site: http://uk.freecycle.org/

When going for a second-hand greenhouse you will probably find an aluminium frame easier to transport and re-assemble. If you have a choice, go for polycarbonate panes in preference to glass for safety's sake. If your allotment site is plagued by vandalism, bear in mind your greenhouse might be a prime target.

**Cold frames**
The cold frame is essential for hardening off young plants such as acclimatising seedlings raised in warmth to the colder temperatures outside.

Cold frames can be obtained from a garden centre or DIY store but they are easy to build. A frame can be made with an old glass window: a wooden frame is built 30 cm (1 ft high), and the window placed on top. The frame needs to be draught-proof. The roof is often sloped towards the winter sun to capture more light. Clear plastic, rigid polycarbonate or polyethene sheeting would be safer than glass.

# TOOLS AND SUNDRY ITEMS

I think most gardeners take pleasure in building a collection of tools to enable them to do all required tasks with the minimum of effort. A good tool does not need to be expensive — far from it. Quite often the most treasured tools are those second-hand gems that have been inherited from friends and family or bought cheaply at junk shops and boot fairs. I have had experience of fairly expensive tools that have only lasted one or two seasons, for example a stainless steel spade that snapped at a weld. Before buying a tool, try to check if it will be strong enough for the job and that it is comfortable to use, being the right size and type to suit your needs.

Here are some of the basic tools in constant use, those that I find indespensible at the allotment and also some sundry useful items:

## Spades
Spades are used for digging planting holes, shifting soil and general cultivation. There are two main types of spade: the standard spade and the smaller border (ladies) spade. The border is designed to be used in confined spaces but can also be good for people who find it hard going using a standard spade. If you can handle a standard spade, the larger, heavier blade can make quicker work of a large amount of digging. If you are over 1.7 m (5 ft 6 in) tall, it would be worth looking for spade with a longer than standard shaft. Some spades have a tread on top of the blade. These treads make it easier to push the blade into the soil but are usually only found on the more expensive tools. Another factor to consider is the material the spade is made from. Stainless steel blades are easy to clean and heavy soil does not cling

as it would do to a carbon steel blade, but they are more expensive. Carbon steel is the more common choice and should perform well if cleaned and oiled after use. The shaft of the spade is usually made from wood or metal. Personally I prefer to use all carbon steel spades as the join between blade and a wooden or plastic shaft is always a weak point. You are more likely to find these all metal spades at a builders merchant rather than a garden centre.

**Forks**
Forks are used for general cultivation, lifting root crops and shifting manure and bulky compost. Forks penetrate the soil easily so they can be better than a spade for digging soil that's heavy, such as clay, or full of stones. Forking is also useful for clearing weeds by easing out roots rather than chopping them up with a spade. As with spades, there are two sizes of garden forks: the standard and border. If you are tall, you will also find longer than standard length if you search around.

**Hoes**
Although mainly used for weeding, hoes can be used for aerating soil, froming seed drills and other tasks. Controlling weeds with a hoe is far quicker than hand weeding. When weeding with a hoe the objective is to cut the weed from the roots at just below soil level. Make sure that when you hoe you are as upright as possible to make it easy on your back. The key to achieving this is choosing a hoe with the correct length handle to suit your height. The top of handle should be level with your ear when the hoe is upright with the blade resting on the ground.

The dutch hoe, which has a D-shaped blade, is probably the most common and is excellent for cutting through surface weeds without damaging plant roots. The draw hoe is good for chopping weeds and can also be used to earth up potatoes and making drills for sowing seeds. An onion hoe is a short-handled draw hoe, useful for weeding between closely grown plants while in a squatting or kneeling position.

### Digging hoes

The digging hoe is also known as the eye hoe, grub hoe or Chillington hoe. Although uncommon and hard to find in the UK, it is the digging tool of choice for gardeners and smallholders in many parts of the world, especially Spain and South America, where it is known as the azada. A digging hoe isn't an essential tool but many allotment gardeners swear by them for digging over the ground very quickly and with much less effort than a conventional spade.

Using a digging hoe is very different from using a shovel or spade. Instead of ramming a shovel blade into the earth, the heavy hoe blade swings from hip height down into the soil using it's own weight, gravity, and a little help from your arms. Instead of leaning over to lift the shovel load of soil with your back, with the digging hoe you use your whole body to pull the thin slice of soil towards you into a previously cleared space.

### Rakes

A garden rake has short, wide rounded teeth and is for final soil levelling, and making a 'tilth' — a fine, even soil surface for sowing/planting into. A garden rake is also used for drawing up and mounding soil, for pulling out stones and breaking up small clumps of earth.

## Cultivator

Looking like a claw, a hand cultivator has three or five prongs on the end of a long shaft. It is used to aerate and break up the surface of compacted soil and loosen weeds. There is also the star-wheeled cultivator with four or five stars that rotate on the same axle when pushed and pulled along the soil.

## Secateurs

Secateurs are not only used to prune the woody stems of fruit canes but they can also be used to take cuttings for propagation and lesser tasks like cutting up vegetation bound for the compost heap. For inexperienced gardeners, they may be safer to use than a knife.

There are two main types of secateurs: by-pass secateurs, which cut with a scissor-like action or anvil secateurs, which have one blade cutting against a flat lower anvil.

Unless you have or intend to grow a lot of fruit on your allotment, a cheap pair of secateurs should be suffcient. Good points to look out for are stainless or carbon steel blades in preference to coated steel. Make sure the size fits your hand comfortably. Ratcheting secateurs require less effort and cause less strain on the users hands.

## Garden knife

A knife is indispensable for most gardeners. It can be used for harvesting many types of veg, light pruning, cutting string and many other varied tasks. Take good care of your knife, keep it sharp, dry the blade after use and wipe it over with an oily rag.

## Scissors
Scissors are the best tool for cutting salad leaves and herbs and have many other uses on the allotment.

## Trowel
A trowel is essential for digging the small holes in which to plant seedlings. Some are marked with gauges to aid measuring soil depth.

## Hand fork
This is a useful weeding tool.

## Watering can
Hoses are not allowed at many allotments, and where they are allowed you may be banned from using them in times of drought, so you will need at least two watering cans (have more cans available for anyone who helps with your plot). When going to fetch water from the supply it makes sense to keep balanced and save time by carrying a can in each hand. A 9 litre (2 gallon) can holds 8 kg (18 lb) of water; use plastic cans to lighten the load a bit. You will need a fine or medium rose to water seeds or seedlings. If you do not garden organically, you may need a separate can that has a dribble or T-bar for applying weedkiller — keep this clearly marked and do not use it for watering.

## Sprayer
Small hand-held sprayers are useful for applying organic and non-organic pesticides and fertilisers and for weedkillers. They can also be used to mist spray and water plants.

## Water butt
Collect the water that falls on your shed and/or greenhouse roof. A water butt will need to be raised on blocks to allow a watering can to fit beneath the

tap. The butt should have a lid to prevent insects and debris polluting the water and blocking the tap.

## Wheelbarrow

A wheelbarrow is essential for shifting large amounts of manure and/or compost to and around your plot. You may also need it to transport plants, crops and tools. A plastic wheelbarrow is lighter than a metal one but is liable to split unless treated with care. Metal wheelbarrows are stronger but liable to rust; galvanised steel lasts longer but is more expensive. If you have to buy a new wheelbarrow and need it for heavy work, get a builder's barrow from a builders merchant or DIY store.

## Trugs and buckets

A fine, traditional hand-crafted trug made in would be ideal for carrying hand tools and vegetables, but they are expensive and unless you already have a trug a bucket does the job nearly as well. A bucket can of course, also be used to carry water and other liquids. Even more useful are the flexible plastic tubs/trugs that come in a wide range of sizes and colours.

## Cloches and fleece

A cloche is used to protect plants and seedlings that need a little extra warmth early in the season. There is a wide range of types of cloche. They are made from glass, rigid and flexible plastics or fleece.

For the allotment, home-made cloches made from recycled materials are ideal. Make small cloches for individual plants by cutting the tops off plastic bottles (the resulting funnel shaped part of the bottle is ideal for placing in the ground to aid the watering of thirsty plants). Larger cloches can be made from old sheets of clear plastic or glass panes.

Fleece can be used as a "floating" cloche, covering seeds sown in position. This has the advantage of letting in rainwater while it insulates the ground. The lightweight fleece rises with the plants as they grow.

## Mulching materials
There are various times it is useful to have some mulching materials available on the plot. For example, If you have a spot that has just been cropped but are not ready to use straight away for the next crop, put down a mulch. Materials you can store on the plot ready for when you need them include manure, compost, newspapers and cardboard.

## Seed trays and pots
Keep a selection of trays and pots to hand for sowing seeds and potting on. There is no need to spend money as this a good way to recycle various containers and packaging from the kitchen.

## Airtight containers
It is useful to keep some resealable containers in the shed for storage of seeds and more importantly tea break supplies. Biscuit tins are ideal as they are not only airtight but also mouse-proof.

## Twine and garden lines
Twine is indispensible on the allotment: you will need it to tie plants to supports and creating cane wig-wams. Tar-impregnated string is ideal. Keep a seperate marking-out line made from polypropylene with a pointed stake at each end.

## Plant labels and marker
The white plant labels from garden centres are adequate for purpose but I find they tend to get trampled on, so I make up oversize ones from wood offcuts. Make sure your marker is waterproof.

## Dibbers

A dibber is a pencil shaped tool used for making planting holes. Have one that is slightly larger than a pencil and a larger one that can be made from a cut-down wooden spade handle.

## Mesh and netting

Mesh and netting is available in various materials and gauge of mesh. It can be used as protection from birds and rabbits, support for climbing plants, windbreaks and for shading greenhouse plants.

## Chair

Keep a chair or two in your shed for a comfortable rest break.

## Clothes

An old rainproof jacket stored in the shed is often required when caught out by the weather, and similarly a hat, spare boots and gardening gloves can be useful.

# MONTH BY MONTH JOURNAL

# MONTH BY MONTH JOURNAL

This section is just to give you an idea of how to plan your tasks to make the most of the months ahead. Of course the exact date is not set in stone, especially as temperatures vary so much depending on where you live. Scotland, for example, would be a lot colder than Devon and their winters generally arrive a lot earlier. Also, being truly British, the weather changes from year to year — one year we might suffer from droughts following a hot dry summer, and the next we may be deluged with endless rain.

My suggestion is to read my calender of tasks and adjust it accordingly.

Although allotment gardening can be labour-intensive, with care and attention there is no reason you can't get a bumper crop year after year. Many of the tips and techniques suggested in this book will help you to achieve bigger and better crops and also help you to extend the growing season.

With careful planning you can benefit from eating your own produce all-year round. This will not only save you money but you will be eating more delicious fruits and vegetables than anything you can buy in the supermarkets. Cloches, horticultural fleeces and greenhouses are all ways of helping to extend the season as far as is possible.

# JANUARY

January is usually associated with hard frosts and cold, biting winds, but of course with global warming, this may not always be the case.

## CROPS TO HARVEST

If the weather forecast is a period of freezing, it might be a good idea to dig up your leeks and heel them into an area of dug soil for easy access.

Parsnips and swedes can also be dug up and then covered with either fleece or straw to stop them freezing in the ground.

You should still have a good supply of cabbages, perpetual spinach and chard.

If you get a nice sunny day, it is worth emptying your potato sacks to make sure that they are not starting to rot. Any that are showing a sign of deterioration should be discarded so as not to infect the rest.

## JOBS TO DO

If you have not finished digging over your plot, now is the time to catch up, though bear in mind heavy soil will be damaged if dug when wet. If there are a lot of dead leaves lying on the surface, make them into piles and refer to DECEMBER for making leaf mould.

As you dig up your brassicas, make sure the stems are removed and turn the ground over. As your compost heap will be slow due to the cold weather, it is not a bad idea to bury some of the compost in the bottom of a trench, together with some green kitchen waste, ready for your runner beans later in the year.

This is the month to keep your plot tidy, make sure any trees and stakes are secure against winter winds and, if you have a greenhouse on your plot, making it safe against frosts.

## PLANTING

January is not really the month to plant anything outdoors, but you can make use of your greenhouse if you can manage to keep it warm enough.

Instead of planting, utilise the time to look through some seed catalogues and decide what you would like to try out in the coming year. Perhaps you would like to branch out a bit and compare some new varieties to your old favourites.

# FEBRUARY

If you thought January was cold, you will probably find February even worse. The only saving grace for a gardener at this time of year is that spring is just around the corner.

## CROPS TO HARVEST

Apart from the leeks, parsnips, swedes, perpetual spinach and chard mentioned in January, you will probably find your allotment can provide you with various members of the cabbage family — early purple sprouting, kale and Brussels sprouts should now be available to harvest.

Other crops you may have on your allotment could be salsify, scorzonera, chicory, endive, celeriac, celery and Jerusalem artichokes.

## JOBS TO DO

If you have been working hard and you have finished all your digging over, then you will not have much to do in February. However, if you have been short of time or hit by a very bad spell of weather, it is the time to finish this job if the conditions are now favourable.

Check your greenhouse to make sure there aren't any cracked panes of glass. This could be an ideal time to clean the glass and sterilise staging as it might be the last chance you get before spring.

Also utilise the time to wash out any pots and seed trays and sterilise them so that your seedlings do not pick up any disease problems.

Your potato bed will now benefit from a generous application of compost or rotted manure. Make sure this is forked in well. It is a good idea to cover the soil with a dark piece of plastic sheeting, fleece or tunnel cloches, to help the soil warm up before you start planting.

## PLANTING

If the weather is kind, you can start to sow outdoors. For example broad beans and early peas such as 'Feltham First', can be sown now for a May/June harvest.

Jerusalem artichokes can also be planted, along with shallots. Shallots, however, will have a better start if you cover them with a cloche.

If you are lucky enough to have a greenhouse, then you could get an early crop of lettuce, rocket and radish underway.

It is also time to sow your summer cabbages, as well as turnips and spinach.

If you are growing onions from seed, now is the time to get them started. They will need about 15°C (59° F) to get them going, so you might like to start them off on a windowsill.

## TO CHIT OR NOT TO CHIT

There is a difference of opinion of whether or not to chit your potatoes. Chitting is simply placing your potatoes in a frost-free place with indirect light and allowing them to produce short, strong shoots to give them a head start. My own opinion is that the process of chitting is not that beneficial, but it is better to get your seed potatoes early and keep them in the right conditions (for example. chit them) rather than buy them at the time of planting not knowing how well they have been looked after. If you do decide to chit your potatoes, then egg boxes or old seed trays are ideal. If you are chitting a variety of potatoes, remember to label them well so that you do not get confused when it comes to planting them.

Towards the end of the month you can plant fruit bushes, especially raspberries, gooseberries and other cane fruits. For currants, shorten the side shoots to just one bud and remove old stems from the centre of the bush.

**FORCING RHUBARB**

If you would like an early crop of really sweet rhubarb, now is the time to cover the crown with a bucket or a large, upturned pot. Insulate the inside with straw or compost to help keep the heat in.
The stalks will still grow in the dark, but the only drawback is that the crown will take a couple of years to recover from being forced.

# MARCH

March is the month when gardeners' spirits start to lift. Everything is getting excited about the onset of spring — birds, insects, animals and plants are all preparing for the season of reproduction.

**CROPS TO HARVEST**

The last of the leeks should now be dug up. Parsnips should also be pulled up in early March, before the ground gets too warm and they try and regrow.

You will probably still have perpetual spinach, chard, the last of the Brussels sprouts, winter cauliflowers, kale, swedes, salsify and scorzonera. You will also need to keep checking your purple sprouting broccoli.

**JOBS TO DO**

If the weather is mild enough, you can now plant your onion and shallot sets. Also if you are ambitious enough, March is the time to establish an asparagus bed if you are starting from crowns.

By mid-March you can start planting out those early potatoes that you have had chitting in your shed.

Jerusalem artichoke tubers can also be planted out during March.

Other crops to sow are:

- Beetroot
- Broad beans
- Early peas
- Brussels sprouts (early varieties)
- Kohlrabi
- Leeks
- Lettuce
- Radish
- Parsnips
- Early turnips

Using a windowsill, propagator or the greenhouse, you can now start off your tomatoes, peppers, aubergines and cucumbers.

Using cloches, you can plant summer cabbages, cauliflowers and early carrots. It is a good idea to place the cloche *in situ* a week or so before you start planting, so that it warms up the soil. You will find that you get much better results by doing this.

There is still time to finish planting those fruit bushes, and they will benefit greatly by having some compost spread around their base.

## APRIL

April is a lovely time of year for gardeners. The soil is starting to warm up and the worst of the weather should be past. Remember though, there will still be the risk of ground frosts, so keep an eye on the weather forecast for your area.

Although April is rather a gap month between the last of your winter crops and the start of the early crops, there should still be a few things available on your allotment. For example, late sprouting and chards, and you may have some early salad crops.

If you have a horticultural fleece, it is a good idea to peg it over the ground a week before you want to start planting. The rise in the soil temperature can make a big difference. You will need to keep en eye on the weeds, as they will now be rearing their ugly heads. The best thing for dealing with these is a sharp hoe. Just slide it back and force along the surface of the soil.

**THINGS TO SOW**

There is quite a long list of things to sow outside during this month, especially if March was hit by bad weather.

Things to sow this month:

- Beetroot
- Broad beans
- Broccoli
- Brussels Sprouts
- Cabbage
- Cauliflower
- Chard
- Kale
- Kohl Rabi
- Leeks
- Lettuce
- Peas
- Radish
- Rocket

- Beet spinach
- Spinach

## DEALING WITH PESTS

If you planted carrots last month, this is the time to take precautions to try and beat carrot fly. This nasty little pest lays eggs around carrots when they are thinned. The eggs hatch in larvae that burrow into the root of the carrot, killing the plant or at least ruining the crop. You can either cover it with fleece, making sure that the edges are buried in the soil, or erect a barrier of thin polythene or fine mesh netting around the seedlings while they are still small. Make the barrier approximately 60–90 cm (2–3 ft) high, because this pest does not normally fly above this height. This is a much better way of dealing with carrot fly than using insecticides, which have a limited success anyway.

On the subject of pests, slugs and snails will now be coming out in abundance, ready to chomp their way through entire rows of succulent young seedlings. If it wise to steer clear of any commercial poisons or pesticides as these are likely to kill beneficial insects and earthworms as well. There are, however, other ways to control snail and slug populations.

If you have the time and patience, you can always put on a pair of thin cotton gloves and dispose of them by hand. It is best done after dark, when the little blighters are most active.

Frequent hoeing of the soil will help, as this will expose their eggs so that they will be eaten by predators.

Try watering in the morning as snails and slugs are attracted to moist areas, and this is the time when they are least active.

Crushed eggshells are also said to be an effective barrier, along with pine needles, straw, sawdust and shredded bark. Protect any vulnerable plants by sprinkling any of these or coarse grit around the shoots and new shoots.

Beer traps are also an effective way of catching slugs and snails as they are very attracted by the smell. All you need is a jar, put it on its side with a small amount of beer in it, and when the slugs come along they will drown in it. This is a very simple and effective method and the bonus is you can drink the rest of the beer that you don't use in the traps!

If you have one particularly bad area that is infested with slugs, there is another quick way of reducing numbers. Place a black bin liner in between your tender plants. Open the bag and place a couple of old lettuces inside, sprinkle with bran and pour a cup of beer over the top. Leave this overnight and check in the morning, the slugs should have worked their way into the bag and gone to the bottom to take shelter from the morning sun. Then you can simply remove the bag and dispose of the pests.

Consider planting 'repellant' species in among your crops. These include plants such as lavender, thyme, sage, geraniums and mint.

**THINGS TO PLANT**

Easter has always been the traditional time to plant potatoes. A great source of food for this crop is comfrey. If you make a comfrey tea and use it to water your potatoes, you should have a bumper crop.

Other things to grow are globe and Jerusalem artichokes, onion and shallot sets and asparagus.

Aubergines, celery, outdoor cucumbers and tomatoes can also be sown now and kept in the greenhouse or on a warm windowsill.

French beans, lettuce and sweetcorn can now be planted, but they should be under cloches.

Now is a good time to plant out strawberries. It is best to remove the flowers during the first year so that you conserve their strength. This should benefit the plants and give you a larger crop in subsequent years. Strawberry plants do not last forever, it is advisable to rotate them every three to five years.

## MAY

May will probably be one of the busiest months on your allotment. By now the soil will have warmed up and everything should be growing well, including the weeds. Watch out for late frosts and make sure you keep a piece of fleece handy just in case.

Depending on where you live, you might have some salad crops ready for harvest. Hardy lettuce, spring onions and radishes may well be available this month. Also winter cauliflowers, spring cabbage, sprouting broccoli and kale should be ready to use. If you have started an asparagus bed, you will probably find you can start benefiting from your crop this month.

There are two main jobs you need to keep on top of this month. Firstly, hoe weeds while they are just small seedlings, this will make your life a lot easier than waiting for them to get established.

The second major task is to start thinning out to give your crops plenty of room.

**SOWING IN MAY**

There are a lot of things you can sow this month. It is worth sowing one set and then a few weeks later another, so that you get a succession of fresh vegetables.

• Runner beans
• French beans
• Beetroot
• Broccoli
• Calabrese
• Cabbage
• Cauliflower
• Chicory
• Kale
• Kohlrabi
• Lettuce and salad leaves (such as rocket)
• Peas
• Radish
• Salad crops (grown in succession)
• Spring onions
• Swedes
• Turnips

You can also sow sweetcorn, courgettes, marrows and pumpkins under cover. As these don't really like starting their life in the cold, it is worth starting them off in pots.

## PLANTING OUT IN MAY

If your seedlings have progressed enough, you can now plant out:

• Brussels sprouts
• Summer cabbages
• Celery
• Celeriac
• Leeks

With leeks it is best to wait until the seedlings are the thickness of a pencil before planting out. Dig a hole about 15 cm (6 in) deep and then drop the seedling in. Water well and allow the soil to fall back in naturally.

## FROM THE GREENHOUSE

• Aubergines
• Cucumber
• Sweet peppers
• Chilli peppers
• Tomatoes

These will now be ready for moving on. You might prefer to grow these either in grow bags or large pots, giving yourself more room for other crops.

# JUNE

As we are now moving towards the longest day of the year, you will have plenty of daylight to tend to your allotment. With the fear of frosts past and the promise of plenty of warm sunshine, there will be plenty to do and you can really start to reap the rewards of your hard work.

Salad crops such as lettuce, spring onions and radish should now be well established and ready to eat. Summer cabbages and early carrots will also be available for picking. Beetroot, young turnips and summer spinach should also be available, as well as early peas, especially if you live in the south.

Your main jobs this month will be weeding and making sure that everything is kept well watered. A good test is to poke your finger into the soil and if it is still dry at the tip, then you need to water. Don't just sprinkle small amounts on the surface: make sure you give everything a good soaking so that the water reaches the roots.

Hoeing will help improve the capillary action of soil and allow any rainwater to soak in, should you be lucky enough to get any.

## PLANTING OUT IN JUNE

You should now be able to plant out your brassicas — broccoli, calabrese, Brussels sprouts and summer cabbage. If you have started beans in pots, these can also go outside now.

Outdoor tomatoes can also go to their final position now, but it is a good idea to condition them before their final move. Take them out of the greenhouse during the day and put them back at night for a few days. This avoids shocking the plant by a sudden and drastic change in temperature.

## SOWING IN JUNE

There are still many crops you can sow this month. If the weather is very dry, it is worth soaking your seed drill before sowing and then just water with a fine spray afterwards.

- French beans
- Runner beans
- Beetroot
- Carrots
- Cauliflowers
- Chicory
- Courgettes
- Cucumbers
- Endive
- Kohlrabi
- Marrows
- Squash
- Swedes
- Sweetcorn
- Turnips

Beetroot, french beans, carrots, kohlrabi, peas, lettuce, endive and radish should ideally be sown at intervals throughout the summer months. By doing this you will have a constant supply of fresh produce.

## IN THE GREENHOUSE

Continue to pinch off the side shoots from your tomatoes and keep a lookout for pests such as aphids, whitefly and red spider mite. One safe way of dealing with these pests is to mix up the following:

1. Crush 2 garlic cloves into 1 pint of water and bring to the boil.
2. Allow it to cool.
3. Add 1 tablespoon of washing-up liquid and stir.
4. Pour into a spray bottle and use immediately.

Now is the time to put netting over your fruit bushes to stop the birds taking advantage of your crop.

Butterflies are also in abundance this month. As beautiful as they are, it is advisable to check the underneath of your brassica leaves for the little yellow and white eggs. These eggs will hatch into caterpillars who will quickly destroy your crop. It is easiest to wipe them off with a damp piece of kitchen paper.

# JULY

On average, July is one of the driest months, so much of your time will be taken up with watering. To help prevent too much water loss from the soil during this time of year, it is worth investing in a layer of mulch of organic matter around your plants. This will probably encourage slugs, so you will need to keep on top of those slimy little critters. Also, remember to keep hoeing.

## JULY HARVEST

Your crops should now be in abundance and you should have a plentiful supply of:

- Broad beans
- French beans
- Runner beans
- Cabbage
- Carrots
- Cauliflower
- Celery
- Courgettes
- Cucumbers
- Kale
- Kohlrabi
- Lettuce
- Onions
- Spring onions

- Peas
- Early potatoes
- Radish
- Spinach
- Tomatoes
- Turnips

When you harvest your potatoes you need to make sure you dig out all the tubers. If you leave any in the ground, they will not only sprout the following year but will become a pest and a reservoir for disease. Forking over the ground a few days after you have harvested is also a good idea — somehow you always seem to miss one or two!

## SOWING IN JULY

Even though you are well into your growing season, there are still quite a few things you can sow in July.

- French beans
- Beetroot
- Carrots
- Chinese cabbage
- Spring cabbage
- Chicory
- Kohlrabi
- Lettuce
- Peas
- Radish

## GREEN MANURE

After cropping your potatoes it is well worth considering sowing a crop suitable for making green manure. Mustard is ideal and very fast growing. Another fast growing crop is French beans.

One of the best green manures for winter growth is grazing rye. It continues to grow in cold weather and should be around 38 cm (15 in) tall by spring from an early September sowing. It will not only give you an abundance of lush foliage but it will also produce a mass of roots that provide humus to help break down any bacteria in the soil.

Here is how to go about it:

1. First prepare your soil by removing any weeds, digging it over if it hasn't been recently cultivated, and then rake it level.
2. Scatter your chosen seeds over the surface of the soil, allowing approximately 50 g ($1^3/_4$ oz) of seeds per square metre.
3. Make sure that the seed is in firm contact with the soil by tapping the surface gently with the back of a spade.
4. The seeds should germinate fairly quickly and cover bare patches within two to three weeks.
5. Leave the plants to grow for about eight weeks before digging them in. If the plants have started to flower before this, cut off the tops and then dig them in.
6. Leave the green manure to decompose in the soil for up to four weeks before planting any vegetables.

## JOBS TO DO

If you haven't already done it, plant out the remainder of your leeks.

Keep on top of the weeds.

Keep your tomato shoots in check. Ensure that they are watered regularly because if they dry out it could result in blossom end rot.

Don't forget to feed your tomatoes well. If you are growing items in your greenhouse, ensure there is plenty of ventilation. If you allow it to get too hot, it can scorch your plants.

Keep on top of pests by spraying them with a strong jet of water. Using a weak mixture of soap and water will not do your plants any harm and will help to reduce the number of pests.

Pinch out the tops of your broad beans as they are the most attractive to blackfly. It is a good idea to plant a companion plant, for example nasturtiums, which attract blackfly. Then you can pull up and destroy the affected nasturtiums and eradicate the insects that way.

Continue to keep an eye on your brassicas for butterfly eggs and caterpillars — these are usually on the underside of the leaves. Make sure you wash the leaves carefully before you use them in your cooking.

# AUGUST

August is usually another month of constant watering. Your harvest should be doing well, providing you with fresh vegetables and hopefully enough for you to store over winter.

Your crop will probably include:

• French beans
• Runner beans
* Cabbage
• Carrots
• Cauliflower
• Celery
• Courgettes
• Cucumbers
• Kale
• Kohlrabi
• Lettuce
• Onions
• Spring onions
• Peas
• Early maincrop potatoes
• Radish
• Spinach
• Tomatoes
• Turnips

## STORING POTATOES

If you have been unlucky and your potatoes have been hit by blight, the best method to preserve the crop is to remove the haulm (stalk or stem) and dispose of it. Leave the potatoes in the ground for a couple of weeks to stop the spores penetrating the tubers.

If you wish to store your potatoes, rinse them off as soon as they come out of the ground and then leave them in the sun for a day to dry off so that the skins harden before storing.

Sort the potatoes carefully and place only perfect specimens in hessian or paper sacks in a cool, dark place. Any damaged potatoes should be used straight away and not stored, as they may rot and spread their rot to the rest of the sack. Check your sacks on a regular basis to make sure that none of the potatoes are going rotten.

## SOWING IN AUGUST

There are still quite a lot of things you can sow in August, for example:

• Spring cabbage
• Chinese cabbage
• Kohlrabi
• Lettuce (hardy variety for winter use)
• Spring onions
• Radish
• Spinach
• Turnips

## PLANTING OUT IN AUGUST

August is the month to plant out:

• Savoy cabbages
• Cauliflowers
• Kale

**JOBS TO DO THIS MONTH**

If your runner beans have reached the top of their supports, they will benefit from having the growing tip pinched out.

Keep on top of the weeds by hoeing regularly.

Keep your tomato side shoots in check, as you will get more tomatoes if there is not masses of foliage. Keep them well watered and fed. Now is the time to stop any further growth by cutting off the growing tip. This is so that the plant's energy is diverted from the foliage into the fruit, encouraging it to swell and ripen.

Keep on top of pests by spraying your plants regularly with jets of water or a water/soap mixture.

Now that the air is warm, start turning your compost heap. The warmth will help it break down and turning it will ensure an even break down. If it has become too dry, give it some water but don't make it sodden.

# SEPTEMBER

By September, most of your crops have been used and the plot is starting to look a little empty. The maincrop potatoes should now be ready, so harvest them and store what you don't need as instructed in AUGUST.

Although your parsnips are probably a good size by now, they will benefit by leaving them in the ground as they taste better after they have had a frost on them.

Your runner beans and French beans will be continuing to produce and the last of the peas should now be ready for picking. You can compost the foliage from the peas, but it is best to leave the roots in the ground as the nodules actually contain nitrogen.

You should now have an range of crops to choose from:

- Beetroot
- Cabbage
- Carrots
- Cauliflowers
- Courgettes
- Cucumbers
- Globe artichokes
- Kale
- Kohlrabi
- Lettuce
- Leeks
- Marrows
- Onions
- Spring onions
- Pumpkins
- Radish
- Spinach
- Sweetcorn
- Tomatoes
- Turnips

Inside the greenhouse you should have aubergines, sweet and chilli peppers, cucumbers and tomatoes.

From your canes you should have blackberries, raspberries and gooseberries, as well as strawberries from your strawberry bed.

## SOWING IN SEPTEMBER

September is not really the month for sowing, although surprisingly winter lettuce such as 'Arctic King' are good for a spring harvest. You can also sow winter hardy spring onions.

Early September is the time to sow your green manures (see article on page 69 in JULY). Green manure helps to maintain the fertility of the soil, which could otherwise be washed away by winter rain. In addition, they will also help prevent weed growth so that you will have less work to do in the spring. Finally, they will help improve the structure of the soil. In the spring you will just need to dig it over and allow the green manure crop to rot down for a few weeks.

## PLANTING OUT IN SEPTEMBER

Your spring cabbages can now be planted out.

## JOBS TO DO IN SEPTEMBER

Continue to feed your tomatoes, peppers and cucumbers. Continue to keep the tomato side shoots in check. The remainder of your crop will not require feeding at this time of year as they are nearly finished.

Tidy up your summer fruiting raspberry bushes, cutting off any canes that have fruited and tying in the new shoots that will bear fruit next year.

Summer fruit strawberries can also be attended to. Cut off the foliage about to about 2.5 cm (1 in) from the ground, clearing and weeding as you go. Any runners can be planted to replace any plants that are now over three years old.

## MAKING COMPOST

Now is the month to make use of your compost heap. Spread the nicely rotted compost on the ground.

As you start clearing your allotment, you should have plenty of new foliage to start your compost for the next season. At the base of the heap place any woody material, such as sweetcorn stalks, so that it allows air to circulate through the heap. Then place a layer (about 15 cm/6 in thick) of green material and add some sulphate of ammonia or dried blood to help add some nitrogen to the pile. You only need a small sprinkling.

Then put another layer of green material, but this time sprinkle it with lime to keep the pH balance. Repeat the process and then lay a sheet of plastic over the top to keep the heat in and to stop if from getting too wet. After a few days the heap should start heating up nicely and be ready for turning in four to six weeks.

Try to cut up pieces of vegetation as small as possible as you will find they decompose quicker.

Your finished product will be rich, dark, crumbly and sweet-smelling.

# OCTOBER

Your main crop of potatoes should now be ready for digging up. As the foliage dies back, cut this off and leave the potatoes in the ground for another couple of weeks. This will prevent any stray blight spores from infecting your potatoes.

The last of the beans should be picked now with the foliage being put on your compost.

Carrots can be pulled up and stored in either sand or peat through the winter. Leave your parsnips in the ground as they will be sweeter if you leave them until after the first frost.

Cabbages should also come up now. They will store well in a frost-free shed, but be careful that there are not slugs lurking in between the leaves. Sprinkling the outside with salt will help.

Any green tomatoes left on your plants should be picked now as it is unlikely they will ripen. You can make some green tomato chutney.

**JOBS TO DO IN OCTOBER**

As each part of your allotment becomes vacant, dig it over and spread manure over the surface. Leave the soil in large clumps and the worms will help break these up as they work their way through the manure. The freezing and thawing of water in the soil during the winter will also help to break it up, so that it is easier to handle in the spring.

Dig in any green manure crops such as mustard that you planted earlier in the year.

Your compost bins will be filling up as you clear the last of the crops from your plot. Make sure you give them a good turn to help with even decomposition.

## LEAF MOULD

If you have trees on or near your plot, very soon the leaves will be falling. September is a good month to start preparing, as these leaves are a valuable resource. Build yourself a leaf mould cage. This is a very simple task — just drive four stakes into the ground and staple or attach chicken netting around the edge to make a cage.

Pile the leaves into the cage and leave them untouched for a year. You will find the pile gradually reduces by about two thirds, so you can keep filling the cage as more leaves fall.

### Uses for leaf mould
If your leaf mould is relatively young — 1 to 2 years old — but it is beginning to break up and can be easily crumbled in the hand. Use it as:

• A mulch around fruit bushes and vegetables
• A dug-in soil improver before sowing and planting
• A winter cover for bare soil.

If your leaf mould is well rotted it will be dark brown in appearance and crumbly. There should be no real trace of any of the original leaves. Use it as:

• A young leaf mould above
• A mixture for sowing seeds either on its own, or mixed with equal parts of sharp sand and garden compost

• A potting compost — mixed with equal parts of sharp sand, loam and garden compost

## SOWING AND PLANTING IN OCTOBER

Although you might think with winter approaching that you wouldn't be able to do much sowing or planting, there are still a few things you can do. For example Japanese onion sets are hardy and will overwinter producing a crop about one month earlier than onions planted in spring. It is a good idea to cover them with a cloche or fleece to get them off to a good start and also to stop the birds from pulling them out.

Garlic can also be planted this month, although it can wait if necessary until November.

You can also sow broad beans to get them off to an early start next year.

## JOBS TO DO IN OCTOBER

Check your brassicas and remove any leaves that have gone yellow.

When your strawberries have finished fruiting, tidy up the bed, cut off the tops, remove any dead leaves and berries that have gone rotten and finally remove self-planted runners.

Fruit bushes such as redcurrants, blackcurrants, raspberries, blackberries and gooseberries should now be pruned. It is also a good time to plant any new canes, making sure that you add plenty of compost.

Take advantage of the next sunny day and give your greenhouse a good spring clean. Wash it down with detergent and disinfectant and give it a good scrub. Clean the glass so that it will allow a little more light through during those dark winter days. Cleaning the frame will make sure there are no pests looking for a place to spend the winter.

If you wish to use it throughout the winter, your greenhouse will need insulating. Bubble wrap is ideal, and don't forget you will need some form of ventilation to stop mould from forming.

If you, like myself, still enjoy eating salad throughout the winter months, you can also sow a hardy lettuce such as 'Arctic King'.

## NOVEMBER

November usually means the frosts have started and it is time to harvest your winter cabbages and cauliflowers. Brussels sprouts should just about be starting and you should have plenty for your Christmas dinner.

Leeks should be ready for eating, but only take what you need and leave the rest until you need them. You may still have a crop of celery, celeriac, kale and kohlrabi, together with turnips, swedes and spinach.

The last of your carrots should now come up for winter storage. Place them in boxes in either peat or sand.

Parsnips can remain in the ground, but if the weather turns really cold it is advisable to cover them, otherwise you won't be able to take them out of the frozen ground.

Jerusalem artichokes will be ready to harvest, and you can start on salsify and scorzonera.

**JOBS TO DO IN NOVEMBER**

Check any vegetables or fruits you have in storage, and remove anything that looks as though it is going to rot before it spreads.

As more of your plot becomes vacant, continue to dig it over and spread manure over the surface.

November is a good month to do 'double digging'. This means digging a trench and then filling it with manure, helping to deepen your topsoil.

Make sure your compost heap is covered and continue to build on your leaf mould pile.

Plant out your garlic cloves, as they can tolerate cold weather. Make a hole in the ground, add sand into the base and plant the clove on top. Fill the hole with fine compose, which ensures good drainage and prevents rot.

# DECEMBER

The bleak days of December are here and most of us are waiting for the festivities of Christmas to begin. Perhaps you are busy buying presents and stocking up on food and can't find much time to get to allotment. With most of the digging done and the harvesting of leeks, parsnips, artichokes almost complete, it is just the Brussels sprouts that are sitting their waiting to accompany the turkey.

Winter vegetables do not demand the urgency of the summer ones, which seem to grow rapidly and need urgently picking.

So use December to relax, knock the mud off your wellies and prepare a journal of what you would like to grow on your allotment the following year.

Happy growing!

# EASY
# REFERENCE
# CROP GUIDE

# EASY REFERENCE CROP GUIDE

In this chapter you will find essential information on all the classic allotment fruits, vegetables and herbs, along with some more unusual and lesser known crops that you may find worth growing.

If you are new to gardening, choose easy to grow plants for the majority of your planting. Build your confidence growing the likes of beans, courgettes, tomatoes and radishes and then move on to trickier, more demanding ones such as peppers, cucumbers and grapes.

There are other factors to consider such as:

• The value of the crop yield versus the amount of space and time required.

• Does the crop fit into your crop rotation plan?

• Can you provide the conditions required for a good crop. Do you have the right climate, aspect, soil, watering regime etc?

• Crops like fruit canes, rhubarb and asparagus require permanent beds.

• Does the crop require protection from pests and disease?

# ARTICHOKES, GLOBE
*Cynara* scolymus

Globe artichokes are not hard to grow but require a sheltered, sunny position and provide a low yield in relation to time and space required.

Pests and diseases: slugs may damage seedlings. Aphids and earwigs can be removed from heads by soaking in salt water before cooking.

Globe artichokes are normally increased by division of established plants in spring using a sharp knife or spade. Plants can be raised from seed but results are variable and it takes two to three years to determine the strong, productive stock so you can thin out the weak. Sow seed indoors in March and plant out in May.

'Purple Globe' is probably the hardiest and most reliable variety for the UK. 'Vert de Laon', 'Green Globe' and 'Violetta di Chioggia' are worth growing in southern counties. As mentioned, growing from seed is unreliable. To grow particular varieties you need to propagate from divisions or offsets of good stock.

Frosts allowing, the plants will be in position for three years and more so bear in mind they are big, 1 m (2–3 ft) across and 1.5 m (5 ft) high. Plant 75 cm (30 in) apart in a position where they will not encroach or shade other plants, but use the space around them to interplant faster growing vegetables whilst they mature.

They will need a soil well enriched with plenty of well rotted manure and then mulched to conserve moisture and keep the area free from weeds. They need a position that does not become waterlogged in winter, and if heavy frosts are expected, the crowns should be protected with a thick layer of straw.

New plants will produce some heads by late summer, but it is best to encourage growth by removing these as soon as they appear. Never allow any buds to open or flower as this will weaken the plant. Pick buds when they have stopped growing but before they begin to open.

Plants that are too old or weak to produce good buds can be used to produce blanched shoots known as chards. After harvesting the heads, cut the plants main stem down by about half its original height and snip off most of the leaves, allow new leaves to grow back to around 30 cm (12 in), then blanch with a collar of corrugated cardboard or a drainpipe. After a month or so you should find some pale stems similar to celery.

# ARTICHOKES, JERUSALEM
*Helianthus tuberosus*

Jerusalem artichokes are easy to grow and are a suitable crop for the allotment.

Pests and diseases: slugs may attack young plants.

For larger, smoother tubers choose modern varieties such as 'Dwarf Sunray' and 'Fuseau'.

They need rich, moist soil to do well. They may grow up to 3 m (10 ft) so plant in a position where they will not shade other crops. Plant in spring as soon as the ground is workable, 12 cm (5 in) deep, 30 cm (12 in) apart. They plants can be earthed up to provide stability and will need staking in exposed positions. In late summer cut the stems down to 1.5 m (5 ft) and remove flower-heads. When the foliage yellows, cut the stems down to just above ground level.

The tubers do not keep well so are best left in the ground until you need them. Cover the bed with straw to protect any threat of frost.

The plant suffers from no major problems but you must be sure to remove all tubers after cropping, otherwise they may become invasive.

# ASPARAGUS
*Asparagus officinalis*

Asparagus is a luxury item in the shop and it could be said somewhat of a luxury in the allotment as well. Although easy to grow, the yield provided over a short season means you need to be a true gourmet to give it the amount of work and time and the permanent bed it requires. Having said that, once you have an asparagus bed it could produce for up to two decades and you will find freshly cut spears far superior to shop bought ones. When mature (four years and older) twelve plants will provide two good portions each week over the six week season.

Pests and diseases: asparagus beetle, rust and slugs.

The asparagus bed needs a sheltered, sunny spot. A raised bed is preferable especially on heavy, clay soil. The bed should be well dug, devoid of perennial weeds and enriched with well-rotted manure and/or compost. Dig in sand to lighten heavy soil.

Start planting asparagus crowns in late March or early April in the bed you have prepared. Dig a trench 20–25 cm (8–10 in) deep and 30 cm (12 in) wide. If you have room for more than one trench, then space the trenches 90 cm (36 in) apart. The soil you have dug out for the trench should be left along its edge, as you will cover the crowns over a period of time as they grow.

About 40 cm (16 in) apart in the trenches make 5 cm (2 in) high mounds of sifted soil or compost. On each mound place an asparagus crown, fanning out the roots from the mound into the trench.

Cover the crowns with 5 cm (2 in) of sifted soil after the roots have been fanned out. Fill in the trench gradually as the plants grow until level. For the first two years, keep the weeds down by hoeing lightly. Water thoroughly in dry spells. In Autumn, when the stems turn yellow, cut down the ferns to 5 cm (2 in) above the soil and mulch with compost or well-rotted manure. Feed in spring with a general fertiliser.

Do not crop until three years after planting and then only for a six-week period. To harvest, cut the spear up to 10 cm (4 in) below the soil with a special asparagus cutter or serrated knife. Allow subsequent shoots to grow into ferns.

Asparagus can be raised from seed, but it would take an extra year to produce a crop. Growing from seed is a good way to replenish your existing bed or add an extra trench, rather than start an initial crop. Sow seed in a nursery bed and then transplant the year-old crowns as above.

Asparagus comes as either male or female plants. Female plants waste energy producing seedlings and therefore modern varieties have been bred to produce only male plants. The male only types include 'Fantasy', 'Grojim' and 'Jersey Knight Improved'. Old-style favourites are 'Mary Washington', 'Connover's Colossal' and 'Gijnlim'.

White asparagus has a more delicate flavour although it comes from the same varieties as green asparagus. To produce white asparagus, blanch the stems with a deep mulch of compost.

# ASPARAGUS PEA
*Psophocarpus tetragonolobus*

Easy to grow and produces a good yield.

Pests and diseases: generally trouble free.

As the name implies; it looks like a pea and does indeed taste like asparagus. Asparagus peas are a good way to extend the season as they crop after the asparagus has finished. The plant also has the bonus of producing attractive sweetpea-like flowers before the pods.

Sow in modules or pots in late April, keep under cover and plant out in late May. They prefer a sunny position in light soil with regular watering. Pick them when 2.5 cm (1 in) long and no bigger, otherwise they will be tough, stringy and lose their flavour. Go over the crop daily and pick regularly as this will maintain the production of pods for a longer period.

Cook the pods as soon as possible. Like asparagus, their delicate flavour needs little enhancement. Place in a minimal amount of boiling water for 5 minutes, drain then toss in melted butter.

Although not a true pea, the plant is a member of legume family and therefore the roots will fix extra nitrogen in the soil. This makes it ideal deal to plant before brassicas in your crop rotation scheme.

# BASIL
*Ocimum basilicum*

In cold regions, basil will need to be grown under cover or in a warm position. It is not difficult to grow if you can provide the warmth it requires.

Pests and diseases: generally trouble free but may suffer from aphids.

There are two species - sweet basil (*Ocimum basilicum*) and bush basil (*Ocimum minimum*), and both are grown from seed. Sweet basil is the most popular species grown, of which there are dozens of distinct varieties including lemon, cinnamon and mint.

Sow seed in March and keep in a warm place, prick out into pots of compost when large enough to handle. Harden off the plants in mid-May and plant out at the end of the month 30 cm (12 in) apart. Seed can also be sown outside in May in the final growing position. Sow in a drill 5 mm ($\frac{1}{4}$ in) deep and thin out to give a spacing of 30 cm (12 in). Keep watered during dry spells and pinch out flower-buds to produce more bushy growth.

The aromatic nature of this plant makes it attractive to bees, therefore it makes an ideal companion plant to plants that require pollinating. Basil enjoys the same growing conditions as tomatoes and sweet peppers.

# BEANS, BROAD
## *Vicia faba*

Broad beans are easy to grow and your own crop will be superior to any bought in the shops.

Pests and diseases: can be affected by blackfly, pea and bean weevils, mice, birds, chocolate spot and mildew.

Sow the seed in soil enriched with well-rotted manure. Autumn sown seed need a sheltered spot and free draining soil.

'Aquadulce Claudia' is the best seed for autumn sowing. Sow in November, 4 cm (1$\frac{1}{2}$ in) deep, 23 cm (9 in) apart. If you have heavy soil and/or live in the north of the country, sow in late March. 'Red Epicure' is the tastiest seed for spring sowing.

A week or so before sowing the seed, add a nitrogen feed to the soil. Dig out a drill in the soil to a depth of 4 cm (1$\frac{1}{2}$ in) and 23 cm (9 in) wide. Sow the seed in two rows, one row down one side of the drill, the other row down the other side. Each bean in a row should be spaced 25 cm (10 in) apart from the next bean. If more than one double row is required, leave 60 cm (2 ft) between each double row.

Earth up overwintering plants to help protect them from the elements. Taller cultivars should be supported by wire strung between strong canes. Once flowering starts, pinch out the growing tips to encourage pods and to combat blackfly.

# BEANS, FRENCH
## *Phaseolus vulgaris*

French beans also known as kidney, haricot or string beans, are easy to grow and come in a wide range of forms and varieties that can be eaten as immature pods, as shelled, half-ripe bean seeds or dried, mature bean seeds. Never eat the pods raw as the seeds contain toxins that are destroyed by cooking.

Pests and diseases: slugs, bean seed flies, aphids, foot and root rots, halo blight, anthracnose and viruses.

French beans prefer a sheltered site and rich soil that has plenty of organic material in it. They have a deep root system, so digging should be to a spade and a half's depth, incorporating compost or other organic material during the process. Prepare the soil a month or so in advance of sowing the seeds — late March is a good time. The main sowing period is May until early July; sow in April under cloches or similar for an earlier crop. Sow seed 5 cm (2 in) deep 10 cm (4 in) apart in rows 45 cm (18 in) apart. The bush types may need supporting with short twigs in order to help keep the beans off the soil. Climbing cultivars will need bamboo canes, twiggy sticks or netting to scramble up.

French beans are very frost-tender at the sowing and seedling stage and if unprotected, will in almost all cases be damaged by any degree of frost. If seedlings are damaged by a late unexpected frost, it is best to remove them and plant more seeds in their place. Water well during periods of prolonged dry weather. Mulch around the plants in June to help conserve soil moisture.

# BEANS, RUNNER
## *Phaseolus coccineus*

An allotment plot at the height of the growing season would not seem complete without cane 'wigwams' laden with scarlet runner beans. They are a good crop for the newcomer to vegetable gardening.

Pests and diseases: slugs, bean seed flies, aphids, foot and root rots, halo blight, anthracnose and viruses.

For good eating varieties try 'Desiree', 'Kelvedon Marvel', 'Butler', 'Polestar' and 'Red Rum'.

Runner beans prefer a position in full sun, although they tolerate part shade very well. Remember they are large plants that cast deep shade over a wide area.

The soil should not be rich in nitrogen, which would only result in lots of leafy growth and few beans. Ideally the planting position is deeply dug with lots of well-rotted organic matter incorporated — this will ensure that the soil is capable of holding moisture, a key need of runner beans. Prepare the soil in February or March. Sow the seed after risk of frost has passed. Where more than one row is being planted, each row should be 1.5 m (5 ft) apart, one seed sown 5 cm (2 in) deep, 15 cm (6 in) apart.

Water the bed well if conditions are at all dry. Unlike French beans, runner beans need pollinating, so grow some companion plants among them — sweet peas are ideal. Flowers dropping off early is a sign of lack of pollinators or of lack of water.

Runner beans grow to about 1.8 m (6 ft) high and will definitely need some form of support. You need to provide a structure for their tendrils to grow round and help pull the plant up.

The most attractive form of support is a wigwam structure — four or five bamboo canes tied together at the top (see front cover). Although the growth at the top may be a bit crowded, it will still produce a good crop of beans. Other methods are to erect a criss-cross of canes, with each pair tied together at the top. Or you can simply put a line of canes connected together with mesh netting.

Runner beans should be ready for harvesting from July onwards and should continue for two months. Pick the beans while they are still young, leaving them to get too long could result in a crop of stringy beans. Pick the beans frequently to encourage new beans to grow. If you get a bumper crop, it is worth bearing in mind that runner beans are ideal for freezing.

## BEETROOT
### *Beta vulgaris*

An ideal crop for beginners, beetroot is easy to grow. It can take less than ten weeks for a crop to mature.

Pests and diseases: birds may pull up young seedlings.

Beetroot is best grown on medium to light soil. A heavy soil should be well-dug, removing as many stones as possible. This crop does not like a soil that has recently been manured as this will cause the roots to be mis-shapened. Lime very acid soils. Either use a site that was well-prepared for a previous crop (such as peas, beans, onions or celery) or dig the soil well the previous autumn and let the winter frost break it up even more.

Beetroot should not be sowed until after the last frost. Sowing can be brought forward a few weeks if you use a polytunnel or cloche. Soak your beetroot seed for a few hours before sowing. Each seed cluster actually contains one to four seeds. If sowing in rows then leave around 30 cm (12 in) between rows. Sow the seed clusters at around 2 cm ($^3/_4$ inch) depth, 5 cm (2 in) apart and cover with soil. After sowing make sure the soil remains damp until the seed have germinated and you can see the emerging seedlings. When the seedlings emerge there may be more than one from each seed cluster — remove all but the strongest. After the seedlings have reached about
5 cm (2 in) in height you can thin them to about 10 cm (4 in) apart.

Globe varieties should be harvested about 7.5 cm
(3 in) in diameter as any further growth will make them less palatable.

# BLACKBERRIES
*Rubus fruticosus*

The blackberry is one of the easiest fruits to grow in cool and temperate areas. Blackberry canes are not widely grown as they were once readily available growing wild in the hedgerows. Today, however, these hedgerows are fast disappearing and many more gardeners are growing canes on their allotments. It is worth bearing in mind that a blackberry plant can last as long as fifteen years, so think carefully about where you want to position them.

Pests and diseases: Raspberry beetle is the most troublesome pest, but they can also be affected by cane blight, cane spot, crown gall, grey mould and honey fungus. Larger pests can also be a problem with blackberries. The main problem pests are birds, mice, rabbits, squirrels and the like and the only effective solution is a fruit cage.

Blackberries like a soil that can hold plenty of water, so lots of well-rotted compost will help. Thorny varieties of blackberry are the strongest growing and 'Himalaya Giant' is probably the best one to choose if your soil conditions are not ideal. Although the fruit prefer full sun to become ripe and plump, the blackberry cane will produce good crops even in deep shade. One plant can yield as much as 3 kg (7 lb) of fruit.

Because blackberries produce their flowers very late in the season, frost will not be a problem. When planting keep the crown of the roots level with the surface of the soil. Dig a hole approximately 1.5 cm (5 in) deep and spread the roots out into the hole. Crumble the soil over the roots and then press it down firmly with your hands. Water well in the initial stages of growth and cut the plants back to about 30 cm (12 in) high. Do not be tempted to leave the canes too long, as this will not pay off in the long run.

Although supporting blackberries, is not essential, they do appreciate a modicum of support. The best way to do this is to put wooden posts into the ground every 2 m (6 ft) and then run wires between them at approximately 70 cm (28 in) heights up to 2 m (6 ft) high. As the new stems start to grow, tie some of them on to the wires.

There are two ways of determining if your blackberries are ready to harvest. The first guide is the colour — blackberries should be deep purple (almost black) and look plump. The second method is to take a berry between your thumb and finger and then gently twist. If it comes off easily leaving the stalk behind, then it is ripe and ready to eat.

Try to pick the fruit little but often to encourage the growth of more fruit. Frequent picking will also reduce the risk of the fruit from becoming over-ripe and rotting, which will only encourage disease. The best time to pick blackberries is in dry weather, as wet blackberries do not keep longer than one day as they start to rot.

Blackberries should ideally be eaten on the day of picking, but it is possible to store them in the refrigerator for a good three to four days if necessary. They are an ideal fruit for jams, jellies and relishes and of course they are perfect for fruit crumble with custard.

# BROCCOLI, SPROUTING AND CALABRESE
*Brassica oleracea botrytis cymosa*

The word broccoli is the Italian word for 'little sprouts' and is part of the cabbage family. Calabrese is a different variety of the same family, which produces green heads as opposed to broccoli, which grows purple or white heads. Most supermarkets sell calabrese inappropriately named broccoli.

Pests and diseases: club root, downy mildew, aphids, cabbage root fly and caterpillars.

There are several types to choose from, but 'Arcadia F1' is one of the best varieties. It is ideal for the beginner as it is reliable and quick-maturing. Because of the large differences in sowing to harvest times for different types of broccoli, it is essential to read the instructions on the seed packets before buying.

Broccoli is not particularly choosy about its site and type of soil, but they do prefer a sunny position. The perfect soil is a reasonably heavy soil that is rich in nutrients and one that has been recently dug. If you soil is lacking in nutrients, it is worthwhile adding some fertiliser and bonemeal.

Do not plant broccoli on a site that has been used for brassicas — cabbage, cauliflower, Brussels sprouts, turnip, kohlrabi — in the last two years as this will increase the chances of getting club root or cabbage root fly infecting your crop.

Having determined which is the best month, sow your seed in lines about 60 cm (2 ft) apart. Each seed needs to be about 7 cm (3 in) apart, covered with crumbly soil and then watered well. The seed should germinate in about ten days. When they are strong, the seedlings should be thinned out to about 22 cm (9 in) apart.

Calabrese needs to be planted *in situ*, as they do not transplant well, unlike broccoli, which is quite happy to be moved. Both calabrese and broccoli are easy to care for and a layer of garden compost around the plants — not actually touching them — will work wonders.

Start to harvest your crop before the flowers open. Make sure you pick both broccoli and calabrese regularly to ensure that the heads are at their tastiest and to encourage the growth of new side shoots.

Both these crops freeze well. Blanch the spears for about two to three minutes in salted water. Drain well and allow them to cool for five minutes and then freeze. The less water on them at the time of freezing, the better. They will keep for a week in your regular refrigerator, but they are infinitely better if they are harvested and eaten on the same day.

# BRUSSELS SPROUTS
*Brassica oleracea*

Brussels sprouts are ideally suited to cold, frosty winters, producing their crops from late October through to early March. They will grow in almost any type of soil and do not mind being in a shady position.

They were cultivated back in Belgium as far back as 1200, which is where they got their name, but today they are available all over Europe. They are traditionally eaten with Christmas dinner, but are an excellent vegetable to accompany any meal.

Having said that, Brussels sprouts will tolerate most soils, but they can be susceptible to club root if the conditions are too acidic. Because these plants are top heavy, a firm soil is best to prevent the roots from being forced out of the ground and also away from an area susceptible to strong winds.

Pests and diseases: aphids, club root.

Brussels sprouts seed should be sown in mid-April in a seed bed outside or in containers filled with compost.

They produce a better root system if they are transplanted to their final position a month or so later. They should be thinly sown about 12 mm ($^1/_2$ in) deep and watered in well. Don't be tempted to overcrowd the seeds as this will result in weak plants later on. The seedlings should initially be planted at least 10 cm (4 in) apart and germination should take place about ten days later.

The seedlings should be transplanted to their final site when the danger of frost is past – about mid-May. The soil should have been dug over a couple of months earlier, in order to give it time to settle. Plant the seedlings (which should be about 7 cm = 5 in high), 60 cm (2 ft) apart. Make sure the soil is packed firmly around the roots and water well.

The Brussels sprouts seedlings are very easy to care for. Make sure they are watered well, but do not fertilise as this will result in leafy sprouts. They do appreciate a mulch of well-rotted compost, and possible staking if they are exposed to strong winds.

A hard frost will improve the eating quality of your Brussels sprouts. Remove them from the main stem by using a sharp knife, as pulling them off can damage the stem. Take the lower sprouts first and work upwards, as the lower ones mature quicker.

If you find that some of the leaves have turned yellow towards the base of the plant, make sure these are removed as they can be a source of infection.

Brussels sprouts are packed with Vitamin D and folic acid, which are both common deficiencies in our modern diet. You either love them or hate them, but cooked lightly in a stir-fry they are delicious. It is the sulphur released during cooking that gives Brussels sprouts their infamous smell, so the less time you cook them, the less they will smell!

They will store longer if they are still on the stalk and can be kept for up to ten days in the refrigerator. Alternatively, if they are detached, keep them fresh in a plastic bag in your salad drawer for about five days.

# CABBAGES

Winter cabbage: *Brassica oleracea capitata*
Savoy cabbage: *Brassica oleracea bullata major*

Cabbages belong to the *Cruciferae* family, so-called because their flowers have four petals arranged in the shape of a cross. They are extremely hardy member of the brassica family and are capable of withstanding temperatures that would destroy many other crops.

Because they are suitable to most temperate climates and soils, requiring minimal attention, they are perhaps one of the easiest crops to grow. There are many varieties of cabbage to choose from but an all-time favourite is 'January King', which has crispy, crunchy heads with a good flavour.

Pests and diseases: cabbage root fly, club root, cabbage caterpillars, wirestem and cabbage whitefly.

Companion planting of sage, mint, thyme and rosemary all improve by being planted near cabbages. A tip to help prevent club root is to plant a stick of rhubarb with your cabbages. You can also twist a narrow strip of tin foil around the stem of your cabbages to help prevent cabbage fly.

The perfect site for cabbages is anywhere with well-drained soil that has been prepared with manure several months before sowing. Plan a succession of sowings from mid-spring until early summer, so that you will have a long harvesting period.

For a mid- to late-summer crop, sow the seed thinly in late winter in seed beds that are protected by cloches. Move to their permanent position during mid- to late spring about 30–40 cm (12–15 in) apart. Make sure you protect them from any severe weather.

Cabbages are quite greedy and need a lot of fertiliser during their growing period. You may find as the plants start to mature that some of the outside leaves turn yellow — simply break these off.

Here is a quick guide to planting the various cabbage types:

| TYPE | SOW | SPACING |
| --- | --- | --- |
| Spring | End of summer | 30 cm (12 in) |
| Early summer | Very early spring (under glass) | 35 cm (14 in) |
| Summer | Early spring | 35 cm (14 in) |
| Autumn | Late spring | 50 cm (20 in) |
| Winter (for storage) | Spring | 50 cm (20 in) |
| Winter (to use fresh) | Late spring | 50 cm (20 in) |

Your cabbages should be ready for harvesting when the hearts are firm. Lift the entire plant with a fork and cut the roots off above the base of the lower leaves. Discard any outer leaves that are too coarse for eating.

# CARDOONS
*Cynara cardunculus*

Both artichokes and cardoons are part of the thistle family and make wonderful vegetables. The edible part of the cardoon is the midrib of the long leaves, much the same as the stalk of celery. Unlike celery, however, cardoon are eaten cooked and not raw. They are perfect for flavouring soups and stews and for centuries have been a favourite in French kitchen gardens, although they are gradually gaining popularity in Britain.

Cardoon benefits from a soil rich in organic matter and luckily are relatively pest and disease free. It makes a wonderful decorative plant in the flower garden and brightens up any allotment. It has attractive silver-green leaves with toothed edges and are best grown in trenches similar to those used for celery. As they grow tall, make sure you position them carefully so that they do not cut off light from any smaller plants nearby.

To plant cardoons, dig a trench 35 cm (14 in) wide and 25 cm (10 in) deep, leaving the excavated soil on each side. Mix a generous layer of well-rotted manure into the soil at the bottom of the trench. Sow the seed in late April or early May in groups of three, 50 cm (20 in) apart and about 1.2 cm ($\frac{1}{2}$ in) deep. Cover with cloches for the first month and gradually remove the weaker seedlings as they apart to appear.

They need regular watering throughout the summer, and a generous amount of weak liquid fertiliser every week. They will have finished growing about mid-

September and this is the time you need to blanch the stems.

### Blanching the stems

Wait for a nice sunny day when the leaves and earth are both dry. Tie the leaves firmly together with string and wrap black polythene sheeting around each plant from the bottom to the top, leaving the tops of the leaves still showing.

Tie the black sheeting in place and then pile up the earth as you would with potatoes. The blanching should be complete in a month and the plants can be dug up as required.

To prepare the cardoons for cooking, remove the outer hard stems and trim off the root ends and any pieces of damaged step. Separate the individual stems and scrub them under running water. Leave the stems standing in a bag of water to which the juice of one lemon has been added. This stops them going brown before you get round to cooking them.

Cook the cardoon in boiling, lightly salted water and served tossed in butter and black pepper — delicious. That is just one way of serving cardoons. Try other recipes or even make up one of your own.

# CARROTS
*Daucus carota*

As long as you get the growing conditions right, carrots are one of the easiest vegetables to grow in cooler climates. They are easy to store, a rich source of vitamin A and calcium and, planned correctly, can give you an almost year-round supply.

Pests and diseases: carrot fly, sclerotinia disease, splitting and violet root rot.

Possibly the best-tasting carrots are the early varieties, for example 'Early Nantes', which can be harvested as early as June. Carrots prefer a light soil that has been improved with lots of well-rotted organic material that has been fully dug into the soil. Prepare the bed two weeks before planting, and fork in a handful of bonemeal for every square metre (yard), ensuring that the soil is dug to a spade's depth and that it is crumbly in texture.

Early varieties of carrot do best in full sun, especially if you wish to harvest them while they are still young. Maincrop varieties, however, prefer some shade, especially in mid-summer. They are an ideal vegetable to be grown in raised beds.

Carrots are best sown over quite a long period so that they are ready for eating from early June to October. Bear in mind that the earlies will benefit from the protection of cloches.

Using a trowel, dig out narrow drills 2 cm ($3/4$ in) deep and 12 cm (8 in) apart. Empty some of the seed into the palm of your hand and take small pinches of seed, dropping a couple of seed every 2.5 cm (1 in) along the drills. Sow the seed thinly to avoid too much thinning out later. Cover the seed with fine soil, patting it down gently. Water with a fine spray and your seedlings should start showing about fifteen to twenty days later.

A quick guide to planting:

| TYPE | SOW | HARVEST |
|------|-----|---------|
| Earlies (under cloches) | Mid-February | Early June |
| Earlies (under cloches) | March | June to July |
| Early & maincrop | April | Mid July to August |
| Maincrop | mid-May | August |
| Maincrop | June | September |
| Maincrop | July | October |

Water regularly, but do not feed the carrots as this will encourage the tops to grow at the expense of the carrot. Remember to thin them out to avoid over-crowding, as soon as the seedlings are about 2.5 cm (1 in) high. Thin maincrop varieties to about 20 cm (8 in) apart and early varieties to 12.5 cm (5 in) apart. Thinning out can encourage carrot fly as they will be attracted by the smell, so try and perform this activity in the evening when this pest is not around.

Carrots that are harvested before full maturity will be tender and more tasty than those left in the ground. If you have a bumper crop, they can be stored in a box of slightly moist peat or sand and placed in a cool, frost-free, dark place. Stored in this way they should keep for a couple of months.

# CAULIFLOWERS
*Brassica Oleracea Botrytis*

Cauliflower is the most difficult to grow of the brassica family. They are divided into two types — summer and winter. The summer cauliflower is what we know as the proper cauliflower with the white head, while the winter one is a type of broccoli.

They all need a neutral or slightly alkaline soil to do well. As with all brassicas, avoid using a plot on which a brassica crop has been grown within the past two years.

Pests and diseases: club root, cabbage root fly, cabbage gall weevil, wirestem, downy mildew.

Summer cauliflower grows quickly, but it requires an enormous amount of nutrients to make the soil as rich as possible. Work on the bed should be carried out in the autumn, so that the soil has time to settle before planting in the spring. Dig the soil to a depth to allow for a good layer of manure or garden compose. About one week before planting, apply a general fertiliser at 90 g per sq m (3 oz per sq yd).

Early crops should have a site in full sun and one which is sheltered from the wind. The site also needs to be away from any overhanging trees or tall hedges, or the plants will be poor.

Winter cauliflowers are much more tolerant of soil conditions and can be grown on almost any type of soil, as long as they are not waterlogged. These grow much slower and require a sheltered spot with plenty of sun. If you have already dug in plenty of manure, there is no need for additional fertilisers.

Early summer cauliflowers that are intended for harvest in late spring and early summer, should be sown under glass from early autumn to mid-winter. They will require a constant temperature of 10—16°C (50—60°F) while they are germinating. While they are growing through the winter they require a lower temperature of 7—10°C (45—50°F).

Second earlies are hardier and can be harvested in mid-summer. These should be sown in boxes, trays or pots under glass at the same time as the early summer cauliflowers. You can make a second sowing outdoors in early spring, although these should be protected by cloches.

The maincrops can be sown outdoors in mid-spring, although you will still need to give them some protection against night frosts. Sow in drills 12 mm (¹/₂ in) deep in rows 22—30 cm (9—12 in) apart, depending on the variety.

Cauliflowers require copious watering and mulching around the plants with rotted manure or garden compost three weeks after planting. When the curds have started to form, give the plants a top dressing of nitrate of soda.

A cauliflower is ready for cutting when the upper surface of the curd is fully exposed and the inner leaves no longer cover it. If left too long, the curds will break up as the flowers start to form.

# CELERIAC
*Apium graveolens var. rapaceum*

Celeriac is a form of celery that grows with a swollen root that can be cooked or used grated raw in salads. The leaves can also be used for seasoning or as a garnish. It is less trouble to grow than trench celery.

Pests and diseases: carrot fly, celery fly, slugs and snails, leaf spot.

Celeriac needs a long growing season. Sow the seed in a seed tray of compost in mid-March and keep in a warm place. When the seedlings are 12 mm ($\frac{1}{2}$ in) high transplant to another tray spacing 4 cm (1$\frac{1}{2}$ in) apart. Keep the tray indoors for another month and then harden off in a cold frame for two weeks before planting out in May.

The final planting position is ideally a sunny position with a well-drained soil that has been enriched with well-rotted manure the winter before planting. Space the young plants 30 cm (12 in) apart with their crowns at soil level, not buried. Mulch after planting and keep well watered. Towards the end of summer remove some of the outer leaves as this will encourage the bulbs to develop. If frost threatens, protect with a layer of straw around the crowns.

The bulbs are ready for harvesting when they are 10 cm (4 in) in diameter. The flavour improves if the roots are left in the ground over winter if the conditions are not severe.

# CELERY
## *Apium graveolens*

Celery is a plant that grows wild in Europe, but is probably one of the more difficult species to grow on an allotment as it needs a lot of attention. If your ground is suitable for growing cauliflowers, then it will grow good celery. It requires a deep, fertile soil that is moist at all times and a long growing season with cool nights. It is worth working out a sowing rota, as the older the plants get, the more susceptible they are to heart rot. A suggested routine is around the second week of February and end of February, then 15 March and end of March.

Pests and diseases: carrot fly, celery fly, slugs and snails, bolting, leaf spot, heart rot

Grow the celery seed in small containers filled with a peat-based compost but leave the seeds exposed. Then put the seed trays in a polythene bag and leave them in a light place. After the seed have germinated, you can prick out the small plants into small pots filled with a peat-based compost and leave them to grow. When the roots reach the bottom of the pots, repot into 12.5-cm (5-in) containers. When the roots have filled these pots (about three weeks) then comes the job of papering to draw the stalks. Use about 23 cm (9 in) of brown paper.

Regularly inspect your celery plants for slugs and remove any split stalks and sucker growth. Make sure that the paper is not too tight as this will restrict growth. Repeat the process, using longer paper as your plants start to get bigger. It is essential that the soil is kept as moist as possible and it helps to spray the plants with a very dilute mixture of calcium nitrate (about a $\frac{1}{4}$ teaspoon to a litre of water), as this will help to deter heart rot.

You need to continue papering as the plants get bigger, but now it is kept to the leafy part of the stalk. Place a cane alongside and use a tie to keep the plant attached to the cane. Your plants should ideally end up between 1.2–1.5 m (4–5 ft) tall and the canes should help to protect them against strong winds. Keep a constant watch for both suckers and split stalks, both of which must be removed.

The best way to lift celery is to insert a spade on all four sides of the base of the plant and then grasping the leafy top, pull gently. Remove the paper and then use a hose to get rid of all the unnecessary dirt inside the stems.

At its quickest growing rate, celery takes around eleven weeks from planting to harvest.

# CHERVIL
*Anthriscus cerefolium*

Chervil is an attractive, ferny plant that is quick to grow and can be harvested in about eight weeks. It is also a hardy herb so you can use it during the winter and into spring from an autumn sowing.

Chervil will grow in almost any soil but doesn't like being too wet, so it won't tolerate badly drained soil. It can be plated outdoor in small pots or directly into the ground in a sunny position. Sow the seed thinly in rows 30 cm (12 in) apart and press gently into the soil surface. Thin plants to 30 cm (12 in) apart. It can be sown any time during the growing season, up to eight weeks before the first frosts appear.

Remove the flowers from the plants before they open and make sure they are kept watered. Pick the leaves just before the buds are about to break.

Chervil is most commonly used with parsley, chives and tarragon to form the *fines herbes* mixture. It is generally used in soups, sauces, salads and egg dishes but can be a great flavouring for most meat and fish dishes.

# CHICORY
### *Cichorium intybus*

This salad plant has a slightly bitter taste and is very easy to grow. It can be sown in early summer and you should have a good crop from autumn to early winter.

Pests and diseases: cutworms, slugs and snails, caterpillars of the swift moth.

There are three types of chicory: red chicory, which is also known as raddichio, the sugarloaf varieties that resemble lettuce and then forcing chicory. This type is not grown in the normal way and is forced to grow by depriving it of light. This gives you edible white growths called chicons.

Chicory will thrive in a sunny spot with well-drained soil and, grown in short rows, is ideal for your allotment plot. It is best to prepare your soil for spring sowing by digging it in the winter and adding plenty of well-rotted manure. Remove any weeds and large stones and then rake to a level finish. One week before sowing sprinkle with a general-purpose fertiliser over the area and then rake into the surface.

Seed should be sown in July or August for plants ready to be harvested from October to December. Stretch a piece of string between two canes to give you a straight line and then make a shallow trench about 12 mm ($\frac{1}{2}$ in) deep. Sow the seeds thinly, cover, water and label.

The seeds should take about two weeks to germinate. When they are about 2.5 cm (1 in) tall, thin them out, leaving a space between each plant of about 15 cm (6 in). Water well and do not allow the ground to dry out as this could encourage your chicory to run to seed. To harvest your crop, use a sharp knife and cut off the heads of the sugarloaf variety. Varieties with red leaves should be harvested after a period of cold weather, as this is when they turn the lovely dark red colour.

## FORCING CHICORY

There are several varieties of chicory that are suitable for forcing, an example of which is 'Witloof de Brussels'. Buy dormant plants in pots in the autumn. In November cut back the growth, leaving short stubs just above the soil. Put a bucket over the top of the pot to block out any light and put in a frost-free place such as a garage or shed. In several weeks tender white chicons will have formed. These first growths can be cut off at the base and the process repeated until spring. After this, take off the bucket and allow the plants to grow normally. If you are forcing chicory already in the ground, then dig up a few roots, put them into 3-litre pots and then treat as pot-grown plants.

# CORIANDER
## *Coriandrum sativum*

Coriander is a herb that grows best in light, well-drained soil in a sunny position with a dry atmosphere. It does not grow well in damp conditions, so be careful not to overwater. Also do not plant too close to fennel as neither plant will do well. Coriander can be grown for both its seeds and its leaves. Coriander seeds are often used in curries and have a totally different taste to the leaves. The leaves can also be used in curries and are nice in salads too.

Pests and diseases: coriander is generally trouble-free.

Plant seed directly in the soil in spring, after the risk of frost has passed. Sow them thinly in shallow drills then cover them with compost. If you want to grow coriander for the seed, they should be planted about 23 cm (9 in) apart, if you prefer the leaves, then 5 cm (2 in) will be sufficient.

You can pick the young leaves whenever you like, ideally they should be about 10 cm (4 in) in height and be bright green in colour. Frequent picking will help improve your crop of coriander.

If you want to collect the seed then you will need to cut the flower stems as soon as the seed start to smell right, otherwise they will fall off and go everywhere. Tie bunches of about six heads together and then place in a paper bag. Tie the end of the bag and then hang upside down in a warm, dry and airy place. Leave for about two weeks, by which time all the seed should have fallen off. Keep them in an airtight container or old jam jar.

# CORN SALAD
*Valerianella locusta*

Corn salad, is also known as lamb's lettuce. It is a salad vegetable that was introduced to Britain about 400 years ago and is versatile as it can be grown throughout the year. It is generally sown as an autumn and winter crop to use when other salad greens are scarce.

Pests and diseases: apart from slugs and snails, this plant is virtually pest and disease free.

Corn salad is a good substitute for lettuce and can be used in all the same ways. If your area is suffering from a particularly harsh winter, then your crop will benefit from being covered with cloches. This will ensure that you have a plentiful supply of tender, young leaves.

Grow your corn salad in a sunny spot in well-drained soil. It should have been dug over and given a generous amount of well-rotted manure. The hardiest variety is the 'Large-leaved Italian', which will give you around twenty plants to a 3 m (10 ft) area. By sowing in March, April, August and September, you will get a fresh supply all year round. Sow the seeds in drills 12 mm ($\frac{1}{2}$ in) deep with 23 cm (9 in) between rows. Thin the seedlings to 15 cm (6 in) apart. Keep the ground well watered during the first few weeks and how frequently to keep the weeds under control.

The plants are ready to harvest once they have produced their fourth pair of leaves. They are quite short-lived, so it is advisable to start using the leaves as soon as they are ready.

# CUCUMBERS
## *Cucumis sativas*

The cucumber has been around for thousands of years and if you enjoy the taste of fresh cucumber, you will be surprised how much nicer they taste if you grow them yourself. If you do decide to grow cucumbers, you will need to bear in mind that they do need a lot of space. If your space is limited, then you can train young shoots along wires, rather like tomatoes.

Pests and diseases: red spider mites, whitefly, cucumber mosaic virus, grey mould, powdery mildew and soil-borne diseases.

Growing cucumbers is slightly more complicated than some of the other vegetables, but I am concentrating on the outdoor ridge cucumber that can be cultivated outside of a greenhouse. It is very-high yielding — just three plants should provide all the cucumbers necessary for a small family.

## Pollination
Ridge cucumbers produce both male and female flowers. The female flowers need to be pollinated by the male flowers for the cucumbers to develop. It is important not to remove any flowers as the insects will do the job of pollination for you. If you are starting them off under cloches, make sure you open the cloches up during the warmer part of the day so that the insects can get to the flowers.

## Sowing and planting ridge cucumbers
You have three options:
• Sow seed indoors and harden them off for two weeks. Plant out when the seedlings are about 15 cm (6 in) high.

- Sow seed directly outside and protect with a cloche during early stages.
- Buy small cucumber plants, harden them off for two weeks and then plant outside.

The ideal method is to dig a trough about 30 cm (12 in) deep and wide. Fill the bottom of the trough with well-rotted compost and then cover over with soil. The dug soil will now be higher than the surrounding soil, so it will form a ridge. If you decide to have more than one ridge, leave about 1.2 m (4 ft) between the ridges.

Where your soil is very light and free-draining, the ridge method will not be suitable as the plants will not have enough moisture. Dig as described above, but leave the surface flat. Place your cloches in position three or four weeks before sowing, as this will help warm up the soil and help the seed to germinate.

Cucumbers should be sown about 2.5 cm (1 in) deep and 60 cm (2 ft) apart. When sowing the seeds, make sure the pointed end of the seed points downwards and water well.

Cucumber plants will produce too much leafy growth and will need to be pruned. When the plant has produces six sets of leaves on the main stem, pinch out the growing tip with your fingernails to encourage the growth of side shoots and therefore fruit. At this stage you can train the side shoots to grow up wires.

As they begin to produce fruit, pinch out the side shoots and one set of leaves beyond the forming fruit, but do not remove any flowers.

Ridge cucumbers require a constant supply of water, and to make sure the soil retains moisture it is a good idea to mulch with well-rotted compost or black plastic. Feed the plants with a high nitrogen liquid fertiliser when the fruit begins to form and continue to do this at two week intervals.

Ridge cucumbers should start to crop from early autumn onwards. They taste sweeter if they are picked while still young, so don't allow the fruit to stay on the plant too long. They are probably best harvested when they are around 20 cm (8 in) long.

If the fruit is laying on the ground when growing, protect the fruit by placing some glass or plastic beneath them.

## CURRANTS, BLACK
*Ribes nigrum*

Blackcurrants are an easy crop to grow on your allotment. They are packed full of vitamin C and are especially good when used in jams, pies and puddings.

There are many varieties of blackcurrant but some which I would recommend are the early 'Ben Gairn' or two mid-season plants, 'Ben Hope' and 'Titania' which has a good disease resistance.

Pests and diseases: rust, aphids, sawfly, mildew, black-currant gall mite, reversion disease. You might also like to think about a fruit cage to prevent birds and small mammals from pinching your fruit.

Blackcurrants are more tolerant than many other fruit bushes, but they do like a moist soil to help the fruit to develop. They thrive in full sunlight, and they should be protected from late frosts, which could result in a lower yield of fruit. Ideally the soil should be rich, well-drained and slightly acidic.

Dig the soil to a spade's depth a couple of months before planting, giving the soil time to settle. Add a lot of well-rotted compost and dig it in well.

The best time to plant blackcurrants is early winter, with mid-November being ideal. They can, however, be planted any time up to mid-March so long as the soil is neither waterlogged nor frozen. The plants should be spaced about 1.8 m (6 ft) apart. The depth of the hole is important when planting blackcurrants, so make sure it is deep enough to take the roots without cramping them. Once in the ground, trim every shoot to within two buds above soil level. Although this might sound a bit drastic, it will encourage a strong root system and sturdy growth above ground.

The most important points about caring for blackcurrants are watering, pruning and making sure they are free of weeds. An annual mulch of garden compost will help keep moisture in the ground and also assist in suppressing weeds. A couple of handfuls of bonemeal in spring around each plant will also be very beneficial.

Do not prune blackcurrants in the first winter after planting. In the second and subsequent winters, they should be pruned to encourage new growth. Remove any stems that are damaged, diseased or crossing over each other. Trim away about 20 per cent of the central part of the plant to leave the centre more open. Lastly, remove about 15 per cent of the remaining old wood.

Blackcurrants are ready to harvest when the fruit are nearly black. Try to pick them in dry conditions as wet blackcurrants do not keep well.

## CURRANTS, RED AND WHITE
*Ribes rubrum / Ribes sativum*

Both red and white currant bushes are highly ornamental and provide not only visual appeal, but take up a relatively small growing area as well. Under the perfect conditions, they grow quickly and can produce as much as 4.5–5.5kg (10–12 lb) of berries per bush.

Pests and diseases: aphids, blackcurrant gall mite, blackcurrant leaf midge, capsid bug, coral spots, grey mould, honey fungus and leaf spot.

Another advantage of these currant bushes is that they can grow in areas that might be too shady for other fruit bushes. They prefer a heavier soil that is not too acidic.

As with blackcurrants, dig a hole that is large enough to allow the roots of the plant to spread. Fill the hole with mixture of soil and compost and then water in and tamp the soil firmly around the plant to remove any air pockets. In spring apply a fertiliser and water copiously during dry periods. It is advisable to provide your current bushes with an annual mulch of well-rotted manure and you should also ensure that there are sufficient nutrients in the soil by applying some balanced-compound fertiliser. These bushes will require pruning every year. All the important fruit is produced at the base of one-year-old wood and on the spurs of two- and three-year-old wood. Every autumn you should prune back the canes that are four years old. By doing this you will only have canes that are going to crop. When the fruit are plump and ripe simply remove the entire cluster.

# DILL
*Anethum graveolens*

Dill is a herb grown for both its seed and its foliage. It originates from Eastern Europe and has a taste a little like aniseed. Dill is tolerant of most conditions and easy to germinate, so is an ideal plant for novice gardeners.

Prepare the soil by digging to a spade and a half depth. The long tap roots of this herb will need room to grow without hitting solid soil. Incorporate some long-lasting fertiliser, such as bonemeal, at the rate of about two handfuls per square metre (yard).

Dill is only hardy down to about -4°C (25° F), so it should be sown from seed each year. Sow thinly in April and then cover with a fine layer of soil. The seedlings will emerge about two weeks later and should be thinned to 23 cm (9 in) apart. You can extend your harvest time by further sowings during spring and early summer.

The only care required is that you keep the plants free from weeds, and you should only need to water if the conditions are exceptionally dry.

In the United Kingdom we mainly use the leaves of dill to flavour food and these can be harvested about eight weeks after sowing. The best way is to cut the plant down to about 2.5 cm (1 in) from its base as soon as there is any sign of flowerheads developing.

# ENDIVE
*Cichorium crispum*

Endives have been grown as a winter salad vegetable in English gardens since the 16th century, but due to their slightly bitter taste they have not really caught on. However, this can be corrected by blanching. There are two kinds of endive — the curly variety sown in June and July and the wavy-leaved Batavian type, which is not sown until August.

Pests and diseases: slugs and snails.

Endives do best in a light, well-drained soil that has been treated with plenty of well-rotted manure. About nine to ten plants can be grown in a 3 m (10 ft) row. Two rows containing one early and one later variety should be enough for most families.

Sow the seeds thinly in drills 12 mm ($\frac{1}{2}$ in) deep and 38 cm (15 in) apart. Water thoroughly, keep weed free and thin the seedlings to about 30 cm (12 in) apart.

**Blanching**
Endives need to be blanched to make them suitable for eating. When the leaves are completely dry, tie them together and cover each endive with an upturned flower pot, covering the drainage hole to block out any light. After about ten days in early autumn, or three weeks in winter, the centre of the plant should turn to a creamy white colour and are ready for eating. Use the endives as soon as possible as the leaves with start to toughen almost immediately.

# FENNEL
*Foeniculum vulgare*

Fennel grows wild in the Mediterranean area but is commonly cultivated in the United Kingdom. It prefers a warm, sunny position in any well-drained soil. There are two distinct types of fennel: one that is grown for the fine flavour of its leaves, seed and stems and Florence fennel, which is grown mainly for its swollen stem, which is eaten as a vegetable.

Pests and diseases: generally trouble free.

When growing fennel for seeds, sow thinly in 12 mm ($\frac{1}{2}$ in) drills in March. This should allow enough time for the seed to ripen in September and October. If you want to grow them for the leaves and stems, then it should be sown in April or May. In both cases thin the seedlings to 30 cm (12 in) apart. Pick the leaves as required from June onwards. Gather the seed on a dry day when they have turned pale brown and hang them in a warm place for about a week. Place a tray underneath to catch any stray seed. Make sure the seed are completely dry before storing in an airtight container.

## FLORENCE FENNEL

Florence fennel requires more attention than the common species. Dig well-rotted manure or compost into the ground during the previous winter and then rake in a general fertiliser shortly before sowing. Make sure you plant in a sunny position in well-drained soil.

Sow the seed thinly in a 12 mm ($\frac{1}{2}$ in) drill in April, thinning the new seedlings to 30 cm (12 in) apart.

Keep the plants well-watered and, when the stem bases start to swell, draw soil around them just as you would for potatoes.

Gather the swollen stem bases for cooking in late summer or early autumn.

Although Florence fennel is mainly pest and disease free, you could possibly be troubled with greenfly. In which case it is a good idea to grow a companion plant nearby such as garlic, chervil or yarrow. Fennel itself acts as a good repellant for whitefly.

# GARLIC
### *Allium sativum*

Garlic was originally a native plant with a long history — and evidence has been found in caves that were inhabited more than 10,000 years ago.

Pests and diseases: onion eelworm, white rot.

Growing garlic is suited to both the novice and more experienced gardener because it is relatively maintenance free. Grow your garlic in full sun as it needs to grow quickly to produce good-sized bulbs. Raised beds are ideal for growing garlic as this helps prevent them becoming waterlogged.

The secret to growing garlic is to plant it in mid-October. Dig the soil well to a spade's depth, incorporating as much organic matter as possible to help with the drainage. Including some sand will help improve the soil further. Add a couple of handfuls of bonemeal to every square metre (yard).

Plant each clove in an upright position 2.5 cm (1 in) below the surface, spacing each one about 10 cm (4 in) apart. They like to be fed, so in late March and again in mid-May, feed the soil with a general-purpose fertiliser. Apart from this your only other task is to keep them free of weeds and water them if the weather is very dry.

Harvest your garlic when most of the foliage has turned a yellowy brown. This should be around mid-August. Gently ease them out of the ground using a trowel to loosen the surrounding soil. Be careful not to bruise them as they will not last long in storage.

## GOOSEBERRIES
### *Ribes grossularia*

Gooseberry bushes are easy to grow and produce a large amount of fruit for their size. They are self-fertile, so one bush can grow on its own if you have a problem with space. They can tolerate partial shade and are able to withstand harsher conditions.

Pests and diseases: aphids, capsid bugs, gooseberry sawflies, mildew, grey mould, honey fungus, leaf spit, rust and scald.

The best time to plant is October while the soil is still warm. Prepare the soil in advance and your gooseberry bush should be productive for up to twenty years. Dig a hole of about 1 m (3 ft) round and incorporate as much organic material as possible. Do your preparation in August to give the soil time to settle. At planting time, dig out a 60 cm (2 ft) hole in the centre of the area that has been previously dug to a depth so that the soil mark on the bush will come to the existing soil level. Spread the roots out evenly and replace the soil, stamping it down firmly.

Once planted they are relatively easy to care for. Keep the soil moist, especially when the fruit are formed. Put a layer of organic matter as a mulch around (but not touching) the main stem at the start of each spring. A couple of handfuls of bonemeal applied in September and that is all that is needed. Birds can be a problem so you might like to protect your bush with some 2.5 cm (1 in) mesh netting.

Prune your gooseberry bush in February each year and try and keep the centre clear of most growth by cutting out any weak or dead branches. The younger growth on the outside of the bush should be left untouched. Any older and longer side shoots should be cut back to within 2 cm (1 in) of their base.

Most varieties of gooseberry produce a fruit that are suitable for both eating and cooking. Those for cooking should be harvested earlier than those for eating. To encourage more fruit, pick about 10 per cent of the fruit in mid-May when they are about pea-sized. In July, when the fruit look ready for picking, take the fruit from the shaded bottom area first and the middle of the bush, as these will be the first ones to stop improving. Leave the fruit on the outer edges for another couple of weeks, as these should get plumper.

# GRAPES
*Vitus vinifera*

Have you ever wished to grow a grape vine? Grapes are still considered a luxury and they are a bit of a challenge, but that makes growing them in your allotment really worthwhile.

Pests and diseases: scale insects, red spider mite, mealy bugs, wasps, birds, powdery mildew and grey mould.

Grapes are hardy plants that can be grown outside in southern England and Wales; in the north they need to be grown in a greenhouse. The fruit need a hot, dry summer to ripen.

The key to getting a good crop is to spend some time on soil preparation before planting. The soil should be dug as far down as you can get and incorporate lots of well-rotted manure. It is important that it is well-rotted because fresh manure will burn the roots of your vines.

Most vines are supplied in pots and when it comes to planting out on your allotment there are two important points:

• Make sure the root ball is not too root bound or has been in a small pot for too long, so that the roots have started to spiral in the base of the pot.
• The planting depth should be just below the original compost surface in the pot, so that the root ball is only just covered with soil.

Ideally the vine should be planted so that its roots

are always in the shade and the head should be grown towards the sun on a wall or trellis.

For the first couple of years you will need to concentrate on forming a framework within your vine plant. This involves training the side branches and tying them to wires or trellis supports. Try not to tie the vine too firmly as the branches need to expand. By training the branches horizontally, it will help encourage fruit production later on. Feed with a liquid fertiliser once a month throughout the summer months.

Although the vine will produce grapes during the first two years, these should be left on the vine but thinned by removing two thirds of the grapes that have formed within each bunch. It is the third year that you can plan to use some of the fruit. In late July you should remove some of the foliage around the grapes to allow more sunlight to ripen the bunches.

## KALE
### *Brassica oleracea*

Kale is a member of the cabbage family and is generally grouped with collards, mustard and Swiss chard. The leaves can be curly and quite ornamental, but they need to be eaten when they are still young.

Pests and diseases: kale is relatively pest free, but can be susceptible to black rot and club root as well as aphids, cabbageworm, cutworms and flea beetles.

Like all brassicas, kale thrives in an alkaline soil, so apply lime after digging the plot during the previous winter. Sow the seed in 12 mm ($\frac{1}{2}$ in) deep drill in

April. Thin the seedlings to about 5 cm (2 in) apart so they have plenty of room to become sturdy plants. Transplant them to their permanent bed in July spacing them 60 cm (2 ft) apart. Firm the plants in with your feet and keep them watered until they are well established.

The leaves of kale are ready for cutting from Christmas onwards. Cut out the centre of each plant to encourage the production of fresh side shoots.

# KOHLRABI
*Brassica oleracea (Gongylodes Group)*

Kohlrabi is a cultivar of cabbage thought to have been deliberately developed for its swollen stem. The name 'kohlrabi' comes from German and literally means 'cabbage turnip'. It's not hard to grow and makes for an interesting crop and ingredient.

Pests and diseases: cabbage root fly, cabbage whitefly, caterpillars and flea beetle, club root, damping off, downy mildew, whiptail and wire stem.

This fast-maturing brassica can be sown successionally as a catch-crop or inter-crop. Sow very thinly 12 mm ($\frac{1}{2}$ in) deep in rows 38 cm (15 in) apart. Cover with soil. Sow white and green varieties between March and June. For a late autumn or winter crop, sow a purple variety in July or August. Thin as soon as the first true leaves appear and continue thinning until the plants are 23 cm (9 in) apart. Remember to keep them watered.

Pull the plants out of the soil when the bulbous stems are about the size of a tennis ball. Trim the leaves and roots, and then store in a cool, dry place.

# LEEKS
### *Allium ampeloprasum porrum*

Leek is a great vegetable for cooler areas as it is easy to grow and very versatile. Most varieties are hardy and can stay in the ground throughout winter until needed. You can sow early under glass and have leeks ready for harvesting in the autumn, but it is really during the winter and early spring that leeks come into their own when other vegetables are scarce and can be expensive to buy.

The best soil for growing leeks is a moist, light soil. Freshly manured soil is not suitable because this will make the leeks too tough and coarse. Do not grow leeks in the same place year after year as there will be an increased risk of pests and disease.Leeks should follow lettuce, cabbage and peas in a crop rotation scheme.

Sow leeks 12 mm ($\frac{1}{2}$ in) deep in an outdoor bed during March. Transplant them in late June or July when the seedlings will be about 20 cm (8 in) high, and trim the tops to reduce transpiration. Using a dibber, make a hole 15 cm (6 in) deep and 23 cm (9 in) apart, leaving 38 cm (15 in) between rows. Drop the baby leeks into the holes. Do not replace the soil, instead water the seedlings thoroughly. The amount of soil carried back into the holes by watering should be sufficient to set the leeks in place.

Hoe the bed regularly during the summer and water thoroughly during dry spells. During the autumn, draw the soil up around the developing stems to increase the length of the blanched part. When you come to harvest your leeks, ease them out gently with a fork, otherwise they might break.

# LETTUCE
*Lactuca sativa*

There are four basic types of lettuce: cos (also called romaine), leaf, crisphead, butterhead and stem. The cos lettuce actually came to fame in England during the reign of Charles I. Many lettuces really prefer cooler climates as they need lots of rain. So the key success factor to growing lettuce is to site them in a position that is out of the full midday sun. If they become too hot they tend to bolt.

Pests and diseases: aphids, cutworms, slugs and snails, wireworm. Damping off, downy mildew and grey mould.

They are not particularly fussy about the type of soil as long as it is able to hold water. Do not apply fertiliser or nutrient-rich compost as this can cause rot. To ensure a continuous supply, sow every three weeks and make sure you read the instructions on the packets as each variety will vary as to when it should be sown.

Use a trowel to dig out a shallow drill 12 mm ($\frac{1}{2}$ in) deep and 30 cm (12 in) apart. Sow three or four seeds every 15 cm (6 in) and then cover the seed with soil, firming it down using slight pressure. If the soil is dry make sure you water your seed well. The seedlings should start to appear in about seven to fourteen days, when you can thin them out until they are 25 cm (10 in) apart.

The sowing process is the same for all lettuce at all times of year, although when sowing in autumn for spring harvest, you will need to protect them with cloches from October to January.

Lettuce is easy to care for and the key requirements

are water and weeding. Having said that they will benefit from a layer of organic material (or black plastic) that has been cut to allow the seedlings to grow through. This will help to keep the soil moist and stop the growth of weeds.

Lettuce should be harvested as soon as they are mature. They will bolt if they are left in the ground too long. When the heart of the lettuce starts to form a point and grows upwards, it is beginning to bolt and should be picked immediately. The easiest way of taking them out of the ground is to pull them by the roots using a trowel and then trim with a sharp knife.

If you are growing a variety of 'picking' lettuce, then you should leave these in the ground and simply cut away the outer leaves from near the base. This will encourage new shoots to replace the harvested ones.

## MARROWS AND COURGETTES
*Cucurbita pepo*

Courgettes and marrows can be raised from seed sown directly into the ground or from plants raised in a greenhouse or cold frame. The method you choose largely depends on the type of soil you have and the weather conditions. Raising plants under protection, however, produces more reliable growth and establishment and also helps to avoid pests and diseases.

Pests and diseases: aphids, greenhouse red spider mites and greenhouse whitefly, cucumber mosaic virus, grey mould and powdery mildew.

If you are sowing under glass, then they are best sown on their sides as this reduces the risk of damping off disease, at about 2.5 cm (1 in) depth.

If you are sowing straight into the ground, then sow two seed of courgettes or marrows about 90 cm (3 ft) apart from mid-May until early June. Once the seeds have germinated, thin out the weaker seedlings. Remember that trailing varieties of marrow need at least 1.2 m (4 ft) of space.

You will need to choose a sheltered, sunny spot with well-drained yet moisture-retentive properties. The soil should be improved by the addition of well-rotted manure, which will provide plenty of nutrients.

If you are planting out young seedlings, then wait until about May until the last frost has gone. Dig a hole and drop in the young plant. Firm the soil around the plant and water it in. Protect young growth from slugs and snails and water regularly. This is particularly important when the plants are in flower and when the fruit have started to swell. Mulching will help retain the moisture and if you have a very sandy, or light soil, then a liquid feed will help boost production.

In cold conditions pollinating insects may not do their job and the plants will need your assistance. Simply remove a male flower and hand pollinate the female flowers — these are the ones with the very slight swelling behind the flower.

Once the plants have started to crop, it is quite amazing the speed at which the fruit form. To ensure a maximum crop you will need to harvest your courgettes and marrows frequently. Always use a sharp knife to cut the fruit from the plant. Do not be tempted to try and twist the fruit off as this can damage the entire plant.

# MELONS
## *Cucumis melo*

Melons need excellent drainage to thrive, so the best method is to grow them in raised beds that are about 1.5 m (5 ft) wide and 1 m (4 ft) apart. The top of the bed should slope downwards from a mound to encourage water to drain away. The soil also needs to be very rich in organic matter and phosphates.

The best method is to sow seed directly into the soil unless you live in a very cool area. If this is the case, start the seed indoors and then plant them outside three weeks after the last frost. If planting outside then place three seed into your mound at about 12 mm ($\frac{1}{2}$ in) deep. When the seedlings are well established, thin out all the weaker ones. If you would like to create a successive harvest, sow more seed every three weeks, but leave enough time for these younger crops to mature.

Melons need heat to provide a good crop. In cold areas it is best to cover the soil with black plastic to help raise the temperature. In warmer areas use straw or dried grass clippings over the top of newspaper. To help increase your yield you can use a drip irrigation or a soaker hose beneath the mulch. Feed regularly with small amounts of phosphate. Once the melons start to produce fruit, take care not to overwater as this can produce a melon with a watery, tasteless flesh.

When your melons are a mature colour, simply wiggle the stem where it connects to the fruit. If the stem comes off easily and leaves a cocave end on the melon, the fruit is ready for eating. Do not wash your melon until you are ready to eat it as this can encourage mildew and rot.

# MINT
*Mentha spicata* (spearmint)
*Mentha pipperata* (peppermint)

There are almost a thousand different varieties of mint, but only about six that are worth cultivating. A particular favourite of mine is Apple mint (*Mentha x villosa alopecuroides*). They require very little maintenance and are easy to grow in either shade or sun, with the only drawback being mint grows a little too well! Left to its own devices it could take over your allotment.

The soil should be well dug, fertile and water-retentive. Because mint is such a strong-growing plant, it is better to sink a bottomless container such as an old bucket into the ground and plant the mint in this area. Alternatively you can dig a hole to the depth of 30 cm (1 ft) and line the bottom with black plastic, piercing it with small holes for drainage.

Mint is sold at most garden centres in small pots and can be planted straight outside after all danger of frost has passed. Mulching the soil will help to keep the roots moist and a twice yearly feeding with bonemeal should keep your mint happy. Remove any flowers as soon as they appear, because if you leave them you will reduce the amount of leaves. There is little else to do now except pick the leaves and enjoy.

Mint suffers from only one disease and that is rust. If you allow it to get a hold, it will kill all your mint plants. As soon as you see any sign of rust — orange blobs generally on the underside of the leaves — remove the affected part.

# ONIONS
## *Allium cepa*

Onions are very easy to grow and have a long storage life, so they are a favourite among allotment growers. With a little planning they can be available for most of the year. They are also ideal plants for growing in small, confined spaces and particularly thrive in raised beds. Onions prefer a sunny position with a rich but light soil and you should prepare the ground well in advance of planting. December is fine for maincrop onions. Dig the soil to 45 cm (18 in) deep, and work in well-rotted manure, removing any stones as you dig. Just before planting, tread the soil down so that it is firm.

Pests and diseases: onion fly, eelworm, neck rot, white rot.

When to sow your onions will depend on the variety you choose. Maincrop onion seed and sets should be sown outside starting in March. If you are using cloches as protection, they can be sown four weeks earlier. Japanese onion seed should be sown outside in mid-August. Spring (or salad) onion seed should be sown at three week intervals from early April to early June.

Choose a dry day to sow onion seed, as the soil should be moist but not too wet. If the mud sticks to your boots, then it is better to wait a couple of days until the conditions are dryer. Dig out drills about 2 cm ($^3/_4$ in) deep and 30 cm (12 in) apart. Sow the seed as thinly as possible and gently replace the soil over the seeds. The seedlings should appear about 20 days later.

If you decide to use onion sets, then these should be planted 10 cm (4 in) apart in rows 30 cm (12 in) apart to a depth where only the very tips of the sets are showing through the soil. Dig a hole with a trowel and place them in the hole with their necks uppermost, and do not push them into the soil.

Salad onions can be sown in drills in a continuous row and then lightly covered with soil. Sow at three-weekly intervals from March to June to ensure a continuous supply.

Japanese onions are sown in mid-August in exactly the same way as the maincrop onion seed.

To ensure a maximum yield it is important to remember to keep the weeds down. It is preferable to weed by hand as onions hate having their roots disturbed. Feed occasionally with a liquid fertiliser and water if the weather is dry, but not otherwise. Apply a mulch to help keep the weeds down and to conserve moisture. Make sure you don't cover any of the swelling bulbs as they need to be exposed to the sun. Cut off any flower stems that appear as the plant's energy needs to go into swelling the bulb and not making seed. Stop watering once the onions and swollen and begin to ripen.

You can harvest your maincrop varieties from August to September, Japanese varieties from June to July and spring onions from March to October. The onion bulb is ready to harvest when the foliage turns yellow and tips over. Leave for another couple of weeks before lifting. Choose a dry day to pull your bulbs, easing them gently out of the soil. Lay them on the ground on some sacking, if possible raised off the ground by 25–30 cm (10–12 in) on a wire netting cradle so that they can dry out. If the weather is wet, lay the onion plants in trays or on sacking indoors, somewhere where it is well ventilated.

# PARSLEY
*Petroselinum crispum*

Parsley is probably the most popular herb as it is a low-maintenance plant. Having said that it does like a reasonably rich soil to perform well. It is a wonderful flavouring, especially when used in fish dishes.

Pests and diseases: aphids, carrot fly, leaf spot and certain virus diseases.

Parsley needs a rich, well-dug soil that does not dry out too often. It also prefers full sun. There are two common varieites — the curled-leaf and flat-leaf — and both varieties are treated the same.

Compared to other herbs, parsley is very slow to germinate because it needs high temperatures and so I would advise that you sow it in pots and keep indoors in a warm room until the seedlings have sprouted. These can be planted outside when they are around 8 cm (3 in) high, adding bonemeal to the top layer of soil. Parsley sown in March can normally be harvested from July to July the following year. A dose of general fertiliser once a month will help to keep your plants healthy.

Since parsley is a cut-and-come-again herb, you should find that six plants will give an adequate and constant supply. It should be picked regularly to encourage new growth. If you want to keep parsley preserved once you have picked it, you should dip it in warm water for roughly a minute and then dry it off in the oven. The best time is when the oven is cooling down after being in use. Crush the dried parsley with a rolling pin and store in an airtight container.

# PARSNIPS
*Pastinaca sativa*

There are few vegetables that are as easy to grow as the parsnip. They are available as a fresh vegetable throughout the winter months, and actually improve as the frost gets to the roots. They can be baked, boiled, or fried and even the leaves can be eaten as a green vegetable. The only drawback is the length of the growing season, although they are one of the first crops to be sown they are one of the last to be harvested, which means they occupy the space on your allotment for the year.

Soil is the important factor when growing parsnips, and it should be rich and slightly on the heavy side. Level the bed off to give a fine, crumbly texture a day or two before sowing.

Pests and diseases: wireworm, sclerotina rot, canker, leaf spot, celery fly, carrot fly.

The traditional time to sow parsnip seed is late winter, but if the ground is frozen you will need to wait until early spring. Make sure that the parsnip seed is fresh as they do not keep well. Make sure the soil is well dug and free from stones. Make a shallow drill about 2 cm ($^3/_4$ in) deep and 30 cm (12 in) apart. Sow one seed every 5 cm (2 in). When the seedlings are about 5 cm (2 in) tall, thin them out to 20 cm (8 in) apart. Water well during the early stages and be careful not to damage the roots when weeding.

Parsnips will be ready to harvest in mid-autumn, but remember frost increases the amount of sugar in the roots and can improve the flavour.

# PEAS
*Pisum sativum*

Peas are suited to growing in cooler climates. They are part of the legume (*Leguminosae*) family of vegetables, which extract nitrogen from the air and store it in little nodules along their roots. For this reason, when the plants have finished cropping, dig the roots directly into the soil where they will decompose and release nitrogen for other plants to use.

Peas will grow on most soils, although they prefer a medium well-dug soil with plenty of organic matter. They like moisture and a sunny area, but keep in mind that some of the taller varieties can cast a shadow over any other crops nearby.

The table below shows when to sow and harvest the different varieties:

| TYPE | SOW | HARVEST |
|------|-----|---------|
| First Early | March to June | June to September |
| Second Early | March to June | June to October |
| Maincrop | March to June | July to October |

Mangetout (snap peas) should be treated in exactly the same way as maincrop peas.

For crops in May, sow First Early varieties outside in February under cloches. Place the cloches over the soil in Janaury to warm it up prior to sowing. Prepare the soil in December to allow it time to settle. Dig to at least a spade's depth, incorporating as much organic matter as possible. Add a handful of bonemeal per square metre (yard) and incorporate it into the topsoil.

Prepare a shallow drill using a trowel and sow the seed 2.5 cm (1 in) deep. Sow the seed singly at 5 cm (2 in) intervals, overcrowding will affect the health of the plants. One method of increasing the success rate is to soak the pea seed in water for four hours before planting.

The most important factor in growing peas is moisture. They must be watered throughout their lives. They will also require some form of support – consult the seed packet to find out their final height. The easiest method of support is to place twigs near the plants, in this way the tendrils of the plant will twine around the twigs for support. Alternatively you can erect canes in a row, tying in the plants as they grow. The plants should be pinched out when they reach the top to encourage shoots further down the plants. If you wish to grow your peas against a fence, then place plastic netting to the fence so that the tendrils have something to cling to.

Garden peas are best eaten when they are slightly immature, as the older they get they become hard and start losing their sweet taste. Harvesting them early will encourage them to produce more. As a guide, peas are normally ready to harvest three weeks after they flower. Pick them just before you want to eat them to ensure that they retain their natural sweetness. Peas at the bottom of the plant will be ready to pick first. When the plant stops producing peas, simply cut off the tops and leave the roots in the ground to compost for next year.

# PEPPERS AND CHILLIES
## *Capsicum annuum*

Peppers and chillies grow well in milder parts of the country, but they make good crops for growing in either growbags or pots. Chillies are related to the sweet pepper, or capsicum, and are grown in exactly the same way.

Pests and diseases: caterpillars and grey mould.

Sow seed under glass in early April at 20°C (68°F), but be aware that germination may be quite slow. Prick out the seedlings when they are large enough to handle and pot on when necessary. Harden off plants in late May or early June for about two weeks.

Plant out in a well-drained, fertile and moisture-retentive soil, 38—45 cm (14—18 in) apart, 30 cm (12 in) for dwarf varieties. Cover with fleece or cloches to provide wind protection and extra warmth.

Peppers naturally branch into two or more stems with a flower-bud at the joint, failing that pinch out tips at 30 cm (12 in).

The main criteria to looking after chillies and peppers are:

• Water little and often to keep the soil evenly moist.

• Feed with a balanced liquid fertiliser once a week.

• Plants will tolerate a minimum night temperature of 12°C (59°F) but better results are achieved above 15°C (59°F). If growing under glass avoid temperaturess over 30°C (86°F).

- Maintain high humidity by damping down twice a day in hot weather.

- Stake yielding plants by using three canes to avoid bending the brittle stems.

Pick the fruit as soon as they are ready to encourage more fruits to develop. If you leave them on the plant, they will change colour and develop a sweeter flavour, or in the case of chillies become hotter, but this will decrease your yield by as much as 25 per cent.

# POTATOES
*Solanum tuberosum*

The hardest thing in growing potatoes is choosing which variety as there are over 400 to choose from. Potatoes grow reasonably well in most soils, but the best results are obtained from land that has been well manured. Dig the ground in the autumn or winter working in compost or well-rotted manure. A fortnight before planting apply a general fertiliser at 60–90 g (2–3 oz) per sq m (sq yd).

The terms First Early, Second Early and Maincrop may sound strange, but it is the term that refers to the time it takes from planting to getting a crop. First earlies are usually ready in around ten weeks, second earlies in around thirteen weeks and maincrop about twenty weeks. Maincrops do tend to store better, but they are at more risk from blight.

## Chitting
When you get your seed potatoes put them in a cool, frost-free place where they get some light but not direct sunlight. A north-facing window is ideal in a

frost-free shed. The potatoes will then start to grow short stubby shoots, which will get them off to a faster start when planted out. Although there is much controversy over whether chitting actually helps with maincrop potatoes, it certainly doesn't help to give them a helping hand.

Frost ia a big enemy so you need to keep an eye on the weather. Usually mid-March is about the right time to plant your earlies and your maincrop a few weeks later. If you do have a threat of frost, you will need to protect your plants and you can do this by pulling earth over the haulm from the side or covering with fleece.

To plant potatoes, make a hole with a trowel about 10 cm (4 in) deep and pop the seed potato in and pull the soil from the sides to cover. If you have a comfrey patch, take some of the leaves, let them wilt and place them at the bottom of your hole covering with a little soil. Comfrey rots quickly and makes a perfect fertiliser for potatoes and tomatoes.

Your first and second early potatoes should be planted about 30 cm (12 in) apart in rows about 60 cm (24 in) apart. As the plants start to grow you need to draw earth from the sides of your rows over the plants. The tubers tend to grow towards the surface and if light gets to them they will go green, and it is not advisable to eat green potatoes as they can upset your stomach.

Potatoes are greedy feeders so a dose of fertiliser once a month when the plants are established is advisable. If the weather is dry keep them well watered regularly, as an irregular water supply can mean you will get a reduced crop.

When you first harvest your potatoes you should leave them out in the sun for a few hours to dry off and allow the skin to harden a little. After this brush off any excess soil and check for damage. They should be stored above 5°C (41°F) as below that the starch turns into sugar and can give them a sweet taste. The most important point when storing potatoes is to exclude light, because prolonged exposure will cause greening of the potato and green potatoes are poisonous. Store them in paper sacks, but leave the neck slightly open to allow moisture to escape. Check regularly for any signs of rot or slugs.

## PUMPKINS AND SQUASHES
*Curcurbita pepo*

Squash is classified as either a summer or winter squash. Summer squash has a thinner skin and is quicker to mature than winter squash. Winter squash are larger and slow growing — their fruit can take from 80 to 120 days to be ready for harvest.

Pests and diseases: aphids, glasshouse red spider mite, glasshouse whitefly, cucumber mosaic virus, powdery mildew, soil-borne diseases.

Squash are prolific feeders and need a soil that is rich in organic matter. They benefit from a lot of compost, as well as deep and consistent watering. It is best to plant pumpkins and squashes on mounds as this will provide warmer soil and better drainage than planting in rows. To make a mound, dig a hole about 30 cm (12 in) across and 30 cm (12 in) deep and fill it half full with compost. Mix the compost and soil and form it into a small mound. Sow seeds 15–30 cm (6–12 in) apart with 1.2 m (4 ft) between rows. Thin to one plant every 46 cm (18 in). Water copiously in dry spells and harvest as they become ready.

All pumpkins have both male and female flowers on each plant and bees are needed to transfer the pollen. When the plant has two small pumpkins about the size of cricket balls, remove all others as they form. This will allow the two remaining ones to reach good proportions.

Pumpkins and squashes store well in a clean, cool, dry place. They are susceptible to mildew, so should be kept on slats and not allowed to touch each other.

# RADISHES
*Raphanus sativus*

The word 'radish' actually derives from the Saxon word *rude, rudo* or *reod* (meaning 'ruddy'). Originally from China, they were a staple food that was often pickled in brine to preserve it.

Radishes are an ideal vegetable for the novice gardener as they are suited to most soil types. They like a well-dug soil to a depth of 15 cm (6 in) with no stones or fresh compost in it. Add a handful of bonemeal and ideally your preparation should be completed a month before sowing.

Sow small amounts of radish seed but often to ensure a continuous supply. For summer varieties start sowing in mid-April and continue at three-week intervals into September. Sow thinly in drills 5 mm ($1/4$ in) deep and about 15 cm (6 in) apart. Thin out any overcrowded plants when they are large enough.

For winter varieties start sowing at the end of July at three-week intervals into September. Sow the larger rooted winter varieties in drills 30 cm (12 in) apart and thin the plants to 15 cm (6 in) when they are large enough to handle.

All you need to do is make sure they are watered in dry conditions and they will be fine. They are relatively disease and pest free, although there is a slight possibility they could be attacked by flea beetle.

Pull up summer radishes when they are young and tender, but winter varieties can be left in the ground until required.

# RASPBERRIES
*Rubus idaeus*

The raspberry is a soft delicious fruit that is an easy plant for the amateur to grow.

October is the best month to plant raspberries and most soils are suitable, but a little preparation will pay rewards. Dig a row 30 cm (1 ft) deep by 1 m (3 ft) wide, working in as much well-rotted compost as possible.

The most common variety is the summer fruiting variety that requires support during the growing season. You will need to place support poles and wires prior to planting. Secure two 2.2 m (7 ft) poles in the ground at either end of the row. Tie two or three horizontal wires at 60 cm (2 ft) intervals to the poles. Tie the plants loosely to the wires when they start to grow.

Place the plants in the trenchabout 45 cm (18 in) apart and cover the roots with soil 5 cm (2 in) above the existing soil mark on the stem. Work a handful of bonemeal per square metre (yard) into the surface of the soil. Firm down the soil by lightly treading on it and water if the soil is not moist. Finally, cut the plants to 15 cm (6 in) from the ground. Although this might sound rather drastic, if you do not prune in the first year in this way the plants will be seriously weakened. Autumn fruiting raspberries do not need supports, so you can allocate an area and let them grow as they want.

With summer fruiting raspberries, the idea of the harsh pruning in the first year is to encourage the plants to establish a good root system. During June if any fruit appear, pinch them off. Although this means you will not get any fruit the first summer, it will encourage the root system to grow. Prune them from the second year onwards by cutting down all the previous year's branches to 8 cm (3 in) as soon as the fruit has been harvested.

The plants need a ready supply of water to produce good fruit and all types will appreciate a layer of well-rotted compost being applied to the soil in February each year. Because the roots are so near to the surface do not dig the compost into the soil as this can damage the roots.

The fruit will not ripen at the same time, so harvesting can take place over several weeks. They are easily damaged during picking and storing and do not keep well. However, they do freeze well if you freeze them spread out on a tray, and then transfer to a plastic freezer bag when solid.

# RHUBARB
*Rheum rhaponticum*

Rhubarb originates from Siberia and is a very hardy, frost-resistant plant. If possible it is best to grow rhubarb in full sun. They can remain in the same position for up to ten years and the soil immediately surrounding the plant cannot be dug, so you will need to keep this in mind.

Rhubarb will tolerate most soil conditions, although it prefers neutral soil that has been dug to a depth of 60 cm (2 ft) or more. Incorporate as much organic matter as possible during the digging because it has to last the plant for the rest of its life. The site should be prepared four weeks in advance of planting to give it time to settle.

You can grow it from seed but this can take a long time to get established, so it is better to purchase a plant from your local garden centre. Plants are available all year round, but the best time to plant it out is in early winter — ideally December. Dig a hole a little bit wider than the plant itself. The depth should be such that the top of the plant is 2.5 cm (1 in) below the soil surface. Fill in around the plant with soil, gently firming it down to ensure that no air pockets remain. Water well in dry conditions and spread a mulch around the plant, but not directly above where the crown will emerge.

Rhubarb requires very little care, but every year after the leaves have died down, spread a new layer of garden compost around, but not touching, the plants. Remove any weeds as they appear, as they can be difficult to get out if left. The only other attention required is to cut off any flower-heads that appear in early spring as the new rhubarb stalks emerge.

Rhubarb that is five years old or more can be dug up and split into three or four separate plants.

Although it is very tempting, do not pull any stems during the first season as this will seriously weaken the plant. During the second season, pull only a few stems by gently pulling the stalk as low as possible to the base of the plant and at the same time twisting. The leaves can go on the compost heap, but do not eat them as they are POISONOUS.

Forced rhubarb is delicious as the stems are more tender, sweeter and do not need to be peeled. All you need to do is get a container — dustbin, box, large pot, bucket, etc. — that will totally exclude the light. Place it over the rhubarb as soon as it begins to show signs of growth. The lack of light and the heating effect of the container will rapidly bring on the rhubarb, which should be ready for eating in about four weeks.

Because rhubarb is such a hardy plant it suffers from very few pests and diseases. The only problem might be crown rot, which is where the top of the plant rots badly and it can be knocked off with ease. There is no cure for this, so dig up the infected plant and burn it.

# SALSIFY
*Tragopogon porrifolius*

Salsify is often referred to as the 'vegetable oyster' because of its flavour. With slender, parsnip-like roots, white skin and flesh, salsify is ideal for lifting in the autumn for storing, or can be left in the ground and lifted as required. In the spring the tender shoots make an appetising green vegetable.

Pests and diseases: generally free of pests but can suffer with white blister.

Salsify grows best in light loam and the soil should be well prepared and raked to a level surface. It is important that the previous crop was well manured as fresh manure or compost must not be incorporated in the soil before planting. A handful of general fertiliser can be raked into the surface when preparing the ground in early April. Sow in drills 12 mm ($^1/_2$ in) deep during April or early May, placing three seed to a station. Allow 15 cm (6 in) between stations.

After germination thin out to leave just one strong plant per station and water well during periods of dry weather.

Roots can be lifted for immediate use from mid-October onwards or stored in boxes of moist sand or peat. The roots are so hardy they can be left in the ground until March-April, when tender, young shoots will appear and can be cut and used as a green vegetable.

# SCORZONERA
*Scorzonera hispanica*

You may not have heard of scorzonera, but it is truly one of the great root vegetables with a unique flavour. It can be spring-planted and then harvested in autumn, but it can also overwinter and be left to grow further. One word of warning though, scorzonera seeds to not survive long, so make sure you get fresh seed every year.

They thrive in any fertile, well-drained soil but like a sunny, open position. Choose ground that has been manured for a previous crop, because like salsify it will not tolerate fresh manure. Sow seed in April or May in drills 12 mm ($^1\!/_2$ in) deep, and if you are growing more than one row, leave a space of 38 mm (15 in). Thin the seedlings in two or more stages until they are 20–30 cm (8–12 in) apart.

Water thoroughly in dry spells and hoe regularly to keep the weeds down. They are generally pest free, but can suffer from white blister.

The roots are ready for harvesting in October and just lift them as needed. They are very hardy and can be left in the ground throughout the winter. When digging them up make sure you don't snap the slender roots. Break up the soil with a fork and ease the roots gently out of the ground.

Like salsify, the leaves can also be eaten, especially when they are young. The pretty flowers are also edible and can be added to salads — they are said to have an aroma reminiscent of cocoa.

# SWEDE
*Brassica napus napobrassica*

The swede is one of the easiest vegetables to grow and is well-suited for allotment growing. It can crop for a long time because it can be left in the soil throughout the winter.

The swede prefers a medium soil with plenty of nutrients, although unfortunately it is prone to club root so make sure that the soil is not too acidic. It also doesn't like being waterlogged, so if your soil is prone to this it might be a good idea to grow swede on a ridge.

Pests and diseases: aphids, cutworms, flea beetle and caterpillars of the swift moth, boron deficiency, club root and splitting.

The best time to sow swede in most areas is mid-May to June, but if your area is warm it can be postponed to mid-July. Mark out a drill about 3 mm ($1/4$ in) deep and sow the seed thinly. If you are sowing more than one row, then the rows should be 60 cm (24 in) apart.

The seedlings should take about ten days to emerge. Thin them out to about 25 cm (10 in) apart and keep them well watered. Also keep the weeds down and that is all you really have to do with swede.

The plants will be ready for harvesting in early autumn. However, if you leave them in the ground until the first couple of frosts, then they will taste even sweeter.

# SWEETCORN
## *Zea Mays*

Originally a native of sub-tropical areas, sweetcorn is easy to grow and home-grown produce is far sweeter than any variety you can buy in the supermarkets. It needs to be grown in a sunny position, but will grow in any soil that has been enriched with well-rotted compost. Prepare the soil around March to allow it to settle before planting. When preparing the bed, remember that sweetcorn pollinates best when it is grown in a block rather than a long row.

Sweetcorn can be grown directly into open ground in late May, but you will probably have more success if you start by sowing in pots under glass in April. Sow the seed two at a time and 12 mm ($^1/_2$ in) deep in pots filled with moist seed compost. Cover the pots with newspaper and glass until the seed start to germinate. Peat pots are better than plastic, because sweetcorn do not like their roots disturbed and you can plant them directly into their final position. Wait until the danger of all frost has passed before planting out to their final position and remember to harden off the plants for a week before placing them in a protected position outside.

Sweetcorn are easy to look after and they appreciate a good watering, especially when they are in flower. It is also a good idea to feed them once a fortnight with a fertiliser designed for tomatoes.

Test for ripeness by pressing a kernel with your fingernail — if they are ripe this will show a creamy coloured liquid from inside the kernel. If it is still watery, then the sweetcorn needs more time to ripen.

# TOMATOES
*Lycopersicon esculentum*

Bush and tumbling types are easy to grow. High yields given the right conditions.

Pests and diseases: whitefly, red spider mite, aphids, blight, foot and root rot.

Where the seeds are sown indoors, aim to sow the seeds so that they reach the stage where they can be transplanted outside, three weeks after the last frost date. They will usually reach transplantation stage about seven weeks after sowing.

Crops intended for cultivation in an unheated greenhouse or polytunnel can be sown in late February.

Seed can be sown directly outside in late March/ early April, at least three weeks after the last frosts.

When 12—15 cm (4—5 in) tall, plant 45—60 cm (18—24 in) apart in well prepared ground, singly in 30 cm (12 in) pots or two or three per grow bag. Plant deeply with the new compost level up to the first pair of leaves.

Growbags are a favoured growing medium with many people but tomatoes can be easier to look after in well prepared ground. They require a soil rich in organic matter that will retain moisture. Regular watering is a key factor to success with tomatoes. It is essential the soil never dries out, in hot conditions and water two or three times a day. Splitting of the fruit skin and brown patches on the bottom of the fruit (blossom end rot) are symptoms of irregular watering. Start feeding once a week when the first fruit have started to develop, but do not overfeed as you will produce quantity at the expense of flavour.

'Gardeners Delight' is a very popular cherry variety because it is trusty and well flavoured. Other cherry types worth trying are 'Sungold and Sakura'. For medium/large sized fruits 'Alisa Craig', 'Alicante' and 'Outdoor Girl' are good. 'Marmande' is a reliable beefsteak tomato that needs a lot of support. The Italian 'Plum Roma' is bland eaten raw but makes an excellent cooking tomato and is easy to grow as long as it has a warm sheltered position.

Most tomatoes varieties are grown as cordons. A cordon tomato has a single main stem from which all the leaves and flower/fruit trusses grow. This main stem is tied to the support of a cane as it grows. Remove all side shoots as these will waste the plants resources — these shoots grow from the leaf axils (between the stem and the leaf). These side shoots can be rooted as a cutting to provide additional later fruiting plants. It is also wise to pinch out the growing tip from the plant when it has four flower trusses (six trusses for greenhouse plants), as this will help the fruit ripen.

Bush tomatoes are more compact plants with plenty of side branches. Each branch has limited growth and terminates in a cluster of flowers. They do not need to have side shoots removed or be pinched out but would benefit from the support of a cane.

'Tumbling Tom' and 'Garden Pearl' are small plants intended for growing in containers and hanging baskets. Their size and nature of growth also make them ideal for growing along the edges of raised beds.

# TURNIPS
*Brassica Rapa*

Turnips are an undervalued root vegetable, that are very easy to grow, tasty and nutritious. It is advisable to plant turnips in cool weather as hot weather can create a rather strong-tasting vegetable. They like a soil rich in organic matter, so dig in a 5 cm (2 in) layer of compost, adding lime if your soil is too acidic. Unlike other brassicas, turnips are light feeders.

Pests and diseases: cutworms, flea beetle and caterpillars of the swift moth, boron deficiency, club root and splitting.

Plant turnips in early spring, four to six weeks before the last frost. The seeds will germinate in soil temperatures as low as 4°C (40°F), and thrive in a growing temperature of about 20°C (68°F).

Sow the seeds in drills 12 mm ($\frac{1}{2}$ in) deep, with 38 cm (15 in) between rows. Thin the seedlings as soon as they are large enough to handle, first to about 7.5 cm (3 in) apart, then two or three weeks later to 15 cm (6 in). Keep the ground well-watered or the turnips may go to seed and the roots will become stringy.

Harvest the turnips regularly, never allowing them to get bigger than a tennis ball. Large turnips tend to be stringy and will have a much stronger flavour.

# DEALING WITH PESTS AND DISEASES

You can try to keep pest and disease controlled through use of pesticide and fungicides but the food you produce will be so much healthier for you and your family if you adopt organic methods.

Organic gardening is about achieving a thriving, healthy, balanced ecosystem and you not acquire this if spray your plants with chemicals that kill and harm all types of wildlife whether harmful or beneficial. Always remember you want a garden teeming with life with the many insects and creatures keeping each other in check.

It is better to prevent problems than try to fix them. Be tidy and practise good garden hygiene. Do not leave vegetation lying around to rot as this will habour slugs, snails, flea beetles and asparagus beetles and other pests.

Healthy plants will shake off pests and disease easier than weak plants. Get crops of to a flying start by cultivating the ground well using compost, manure, organic fertiliser or lime where required. Keep plants watered because thirsty plants are weakened.

Use physical barriers to protect plants, for example, horticultural fleece is an excellent way of stopping carrot fly and collars are the best way to stop cabbage root fly.

Use scents to repel pests. Garlic, tobacco, rhubarb and other strong smelling substances are used to repel pests. Fish-based fertilisers not only feed the crops but the smell also drives away many pests (they may also drive away your neighbour).

Use companion plants. There are many flowering plants that you can grow around your allotment that will benefit the ecosystem. Poached egg plant and marigolds attract hoverflies, which eat aphids. Fennel attracts ladybirds, which is another enemy of aphids.

The crops themselves can be companion plants. Plant onions next to carrots and this will mask the smell of the carrots and prevent the carrot fly from finding them.

If you have a problem with ants, aphids, caterpillars, grubs or bugs, try garlic fire spray. This is a homemade organic pesticide consisting of garlic, chilli peppers, soap, vegetable oil and water. A suggested starting recipe follows, but experiment with quantities:

* 10 cloves garlic
* 10 small chillies
* 1 tablespoon vegetable oil
* 1 litre water
* 1 teaspoon liquid washing-up soap

Put the whole lot into a blender and liquidise, then strain through muslin, a coffee filter or similar. Pour what you need into a spray bottle for use and keep the rest in labelled jars with lids. Bear in mind that although this mixture is not harmful to your health it will kill many insects, including beneficial ones such as ladybirds, so be selective about where you spray it.

For more in depth information about organic pest and disease control, you can refer to my other book in this series *Organic Gardening*.